The Quest
and Character
of a
UNITED
CHURCH

The Quest
and Character
of a
UNITED
CHURCH

Winfred Ernest Garrison

₰

ABINGDON PRESS

New York   *Nashville*

THE QUEST AND CHARACTER OF A UNITED CHURCH

Copyright © MCMLVII by Abingdon Press

Library of Congress Catalog Card Number: 57-9785

SET UP, PRINTED, AND BOUND BY THE
PARTHENON PRESS, AT NASHVILLE,
TENNESSEE, UNITED STATES OF AMERICA

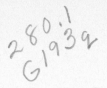
PREFACE

ONE SUNDAY AFTERNOON IN OXFORD IN 1937 I MADE A CALL
with two friends, George Buckner and Joe Todd, on an elderly
couple who were lay leaders of a small and very exclusive communion. Our coming had been heralded, or at least hinted at,
in advance, and we were welcomed with a hospitality which it
is still a delight to remember. A touch of disappointment was
evident, however, when the lady said, "We thought you might
be some of the brothers." We told her we were, though in a
wider sense than she meant.

My first lessons in ecumenicity came from my father, Dr.
J. H. Garrison, who for sixty years was editor and editor emer-
itus of what would be conventionally called a denominational
paper. I cannot remember the time when he was not talking
about Christian unity and practicing it at every opportunity.
In our communion a couple of generations ago the title most
commonly given to "our" preachers (and to active laymen
also) was "Brother." He recognized no such restriction. Some
of his closest friends were ministers of various denominations.
He called them all "Brother"—and meant it. Our communion,
deeply committed to the objective of Christian unity and critical of the denominational system, thought it could escape the
curse by refusing to call itself a denomination. It preferred to
say "our brotherhood." My father was opposed to narrowing
the denotation of that noble word. Call the adherents of a
particular movement what you would, but save "brotherhood"

5

to denote all the followers of Christ, whatever their creed or family of faith.

It is out of this background that I have come to such convictions as I hold in regard to the fellowship of Christians and the unity of the Church. Perhaps it is for this reason that I approach it, not as a problem of ecclesiastical diplomacy, institutional consolidation, or theological adjustment, but primarily as one of clearing the way for the promotion of the sense of true brotherhood among all Christians and the corresponding attitudes and procedures.

The suggestions which will emerge toward the end of this book are really not as radical as they may sound. It is not proposed that the existing denominational machinery be scrapped. The Church must have apparatus and institutions to carry on its work, and its necessary agencies must have constituencies sufficiently loyal to them to make them effective. Like-minded Christians will always tend to flock together when they have free choice and to concentrate their support on those institutions which most win their approval. The question is whether a particular complex of favored institutions with their supporting constituencies is to be regarded as their "church," while all the rest of the Christian world is alien ground.

What I am really saying is that all those who regard Jesus as Lord are actually members of his Church and are within one brotherhood and fellowship, and that all other arrangements and relationships among individuals and groups are secondary to this dominating truth and should be designed in the light of a vivid realization of it. History supports, I think, the thesis that no other kind of Christian unity is possible or, for that matter, adequately Christian.

Thanks are due and are hereby rendered to the publishers and authors who kindly permitted quotation from copyrighted material as indicated by footnotes in the ensuing chapters.

I wish to thank my previous publishers for kindly permitting me to make some slight borrowings from two of my own books that are now out of print, *Religon Follows the Frontier* (Harper, 1931) and *Intolerance* (Round Table Press, 1934), and from one more recent book that is still current, *Christian Unity and Disciples of Christ* (Bethany Press, 1955). If other obligations have been incurred that are not here recorded, the omission is by inadvertence, and due acknowledgment will be made at the earliest opportunity.

WINFRED E. GARRISON

University of Houston
Houston, Texas

CONTENTS

9

Introduction

THE TIME HAS COME FOR ALL PERSONS WHO ARE SERIOUSLY committed to the ideal of a united Church to face realistically the question as to what they mean by a united Church. There are those who know exactly what they mean. There are many others whose spirit is fraternal but whose ideas are vague. It is true, but indecisive, to say that, as the Church itself is not a human construct, so the attainment of a united Church must be the work of the Spirit of God and not the result of man's ingenuity or of ecclesiastical diplomacy backed by theological argument. But the Spirit of God works through men, and men cannot evade the responsibility of making their own decisions as to whether any proposed course of action is or is not a dictate of the Spirit.

This book is addressed primarily to those who are not quite sure what they mean by a united Church, with the warning that if they do not do something toward clarifying their ideas on the subject, they may find themselves swept along by those whose ideas are already clear to conclusions which they will presently find to be untenable. Secondarily it is addressed to those whose ideas about the essentials of a united Church are already clear, to invite a reconsideration of their program and pattern in the light of Scripture, history, and present conditions.

I am not so audacious as to think that I can singlehandedly produce a blueprint of the united Church. I do, however, hope

11

to set up a guidepost pointing in that direction and indicating an open road to that end. It is a road not without difficulties and dangers, and the separated churches may not easily be persuaded to follow it. But it is an open road which, if they have the will to unity, they can follow without giving up anything they cherish except their separateness.

The modern "ecumenical movement" is now over forty years old, if its beginning is reckoned from the World Missionary Conference at Edinburgh in 1910. From this flowed the two streams of "Life and Work" and "Faith and Order" the confluence of which formed the World Council of Churches in 1948. Within these four decades there have been many conferences, countless meetings of commissions and committees, extended and repeated discussions of areas of agreement and points of disagreement among the churches, and fruitful co-operative activities of many kinds and for many purposes. Paralleling these manifold recognitions of the reality and the responsibilities of the universal Church on a world scale, there has been a vast development of councils of churches in limited areas, from municipal to national, and of interdenominational agencies charged with the co-ordination of missionary, educational, benevolent, and other forms of work.

All this has produced three very valuable results: first, more intimate acquaintance and a more genuine sense of Christian brotherliness across sectarian barriers; second, some habits and techniques of co-operation in practical service, in thinking together on the deepest problems that confront man in the contemporary world, and in common worship; and third, a better understanding by each group of the convictions and traditions of all the others. This is clear gain.

The first two of these results have tended to draw the sundered churches closer together in heart, mind, and action. The third—although understanding is always good in itself— has had the effect of revealing more clearly the reasons why they are separated. In dissipating "prejudice," which is always an emotional and irrational barrier among groups, it has clarified and illuminated the substantial grounds for the division of Christendom into sects. These grounds for division are the wide differences of conviction and tradition among the separate groups. The more thoroughly they are understood, the more substantial they seem. Their rootage is both historical and rational. These differences cannot be ignored out of mere friendliness and good will. They cannot be compromised. Their removal cannot be a mere by-product of co-operative action in the promotion of common interests. These admirable attitudes and processes have the happy effect of lessening the social and spiritual distance between the parts of the divided Church, but do not unite them. They never can. The approximation is in itself salutary and laudable, but there is a limit beyond which it cannot pass. It strikes a solid barrier of convictions, and there it stops.

It follows that only one or the other of two things can ever make possible a united Church. The first is that the "differences" which now constitute barriers shall be turned into agreements upon the points that are now at issue among the denominations. The second is that the differences shall remain as differences of opinion, conviction, and practice, but shall be so conceived that they shall no longer constitute barriers to unity among those who hold them.

The first of these two alternative processes would produce a relatively homogeneous united Church. The second would produce a Church united but diversified.

In this book I shall try to show that the first of these programs has not a chance of success, that it has been tried more continuously and has failed more disastrously and more inevitably than anything else the church has tried to do, and that the second method did work for a while, until the church itself scuttled it, and might work again.

The Church never had even approximate uniformity without violent compulsion. It tried compulsory uniformity and got centuries of persecution, the Inquisition, and an explosion. It reluctantly tried civil liberty in religion—that is, the legal right of dissent and separation—combined with the demand for uniformity within each several segment of the Church, and it got sectarianism. It has never on any large scale tried liberty *in* the Church. I am proposing that we try it now.

Much of the argument for this proposal is drawn from history. It will be necessary to show how central the concept of the oneness of the Church has been through most of the Christian centuries, what kind of unity was sought and by what methods, to what extent and how it was attained, and why it broke down. Some modern phases of history will show that the problem of unity has taken on new meaning in our age, so that we face not only the sheer impossibility of restoring the kind of unity that existed (more or less) before the Renaissance but also an unprecedented opportunity to make a fresh start in a different way.

A good deal is said in these pages about the use of violence and persecution by both Catholics and Protestants. Though the main facts are well known, it is usual to cast the mantle of charity over this part of the record and to let it pass as merely a regrettable expression of the "spirit of those times." That is a poor excuse, for the Church more than any other factor was responsible for the spirit of the times. Readers may ask, Why dig up all these dead bones and revive old quarrels? I do not dwell upon this gruesome and gory phase of history in order to cast blame upon any but because it is an essential and neglected part of the story of the concept and quest of a united Church. It reveals the concept of unity that was long held and the means adopted for realizing it. It is therefore related to the total problem of unity and in ways that have not heretofore been adequately recognized.

It will be evident throughout this book, and especially in the last chapter, that the united Church here advocated is very inclusive. It is possible to be too doctrinaire and absolutistic about such a Church, just as it is about the sharply drawn limits of a Church that required a strict conformity to fixed standards. In and around such a church as is here described—

a Church without the usual doctrinal or organizational criteria and without any centralized legislative, judicial, or executive authorities to establish or enforce them—there will doubtless always be marginal groups and individuals concerning which it will be hard to say whether they are in or out. Who has the right to decide, and how important is it that a decision be made? Certainly none can be considered *in* that wants to be *out,* and none ought to be entirely out that wishes to be regarded as in. But the black-or-white fallacy must not be allowed to corrupt our thinking and lure us into believing that the unity of the Church means nothing because an exact line of demarcation cannot be drawn around it with a crow's quill pen.

As I was finishing this manuscript, a radio voice (on "Invitation to Learning") was saying that the first-century Christians "lived conspicuously" because their relation to God in Christ, finding expression in their way of life and in their relations to men, contrasted so vividly with the mores of the society around them. It may be that when Christians embody and manifest their Christianity more completely, their unity and its manifestation will take care of themselves.

The Church has had unity (of a sort and to a degree) without liberty. It has had civil liberty (in some countries) without unity. The motto of this book is: Complete liberty and union, now and forever, one and inseparable.

use this as a conclusion

Chapter I

Principles and Assumptions

IN CARRYING OUT THE MAJOR PURPOSE WHICH HAS BEEN AN-
nounced in the Introduction, it will be necessary to attempt
three things:

First, to exalt the ideal of the unity of the Church and to
hold it in mind as an objective not easily to be attained but
never to be despaired of;

Second, to trace, though only in its broadest outlines, the
history of the concept of a united Church and of the efforts
that have been made to realize it;

Third, to put the present unitive enterprises and the whole
current ecumenical movement into their historical setting and
show how they are related to the social and cultural situation
in our own time, so as to discover what conditions are essential
to a united Church in the modern world and, correlatively,
what shortcuts and pitfalls are to be avoided if the whole
project is not to be wrecked.

In these troubled years of international tension men of
good will have given much thought to the conditions of what
they call a "just and durable peace," knowing that there might
be something that would look like peace, at least for a while,
but which would not be just and, because not just, would not
be durable. Similarly, those who are concerned about the unity
of the Church must give thought to a just and durable unity.
That is why clever ecclesiastical diplomacy and theological

subtlety can have no place in the program. And it is why the word "liberty" will loom so large in this discussion.

Liberty and unity are key words in all the important aspects of modern life—in the political, the social, and the economic orders, in cultural and intellectual activities, in the inmost places of the personality and soul of the individual, and in both personal and institutional religion. Liberty and unity— you do not go far in any direction without finding a place where one of these is being sacrificed in the pursuit of the other. But the sacrifice of either is dangerous. The suppression of liberty breeds rebellion, as well it ought; and the breach of unity where there should be unity brings weakness, disorder, and decay. Our theme has to do with this polarity in the life of the Church—this tension, or "dialectic" (to use that beautiful and impressive word), between the urge to liberty and the need of unity.

Some will say that truth is a category superior to those of either liberty or unity, that the only stable unity is unity on the truth, and that "true liberty" is only liberty to believe what is true and to act accordingly. Truth is indeed not to be disparaged in this or in any other connection, and I trust it will presently appear that due account is being taken of the categorical imperative to seek and cherish the truth. At this point I will only say that, while devotion to truth is prerequisite to intellectual integrity and a prior condition of any fruitful conversation about religion or anything else, the proclamation of such devotion is not in itself a significant step in the direction of a united Church. Every sect in the history of Christianity (granting the exception of a few that may have had less worthy motivation) has sprung from devotion to what was believed to be truth linked with unwillingness to hold fellowship with those who believed something different to be the truth.

What has been said defines the approach to the question of Christian unity in the present discussion. Liberty will be emphasized because it is the factor that has been too much neglected by most of the ardent advocates of unity. If a good many historical facts are cited, it will be because history proves, more convincingly than any amount of argument can, that when liberty is sacrificed, something always happens that is much worse than the loss of unity—and then unity is lost too, for liberty inevitably reasserts itself.

The sobering fact is that by far the greater part of all the unity that men have ever succeeded in attaining has been created by some form of tyranny—political, military, intellectual, spiritual, ecclesiastical, economic—or by the coercion of custom. This has been true of communities of every size from the family to the empire (and sometimes of the family itself) and in all kinds of social structures. It has been conspicuously true of the Church. The whole ecumenical movement will be going up a blind alley if it tries to recover a unity based upon or involving any of these old tyrannies. But if it demands the rights and accepts the risks of liberty, it is on an open road toward its goal. It may not reach that goal, but this is its only chance.

Near the end of my active professional life as a teacher of church history, I gained two insights which have been very valuable in my subsequent thinking. One of these has some bearing on our theme; the other is central to it.

The first of these discoveries is that religious liberty in the ordinary sense of that term is simply a special case under civil liberty. This means that if a man has such civil liberties as are guaranteed by the Bill of Rights of the American Constitution—the rights to think, speak, print, teach, assemble, organize, and hold property—then he has the right to do all these things in the area of his religion and for its practice and propagation. That takes care of religious liberty for the individual. And since the right to organize and to do these things collectively is included in the right to do them at all, it also takes care of it for the Church. Neither the Christian man nor the Christian Church nor any part of it needs any other kind of religious liberty, as against either action or nonaction by

19

the state, than that which civil liberty involves. Furthermore, without a reliable guarantee of general civil liberty including the rights above specified, any so-called religious liberty is merely a grant of privilege, insecurely based and precariously held. The Church, therefore, has a specific interest in universal civil liberty. The American Bill of Rights is cited only because it is the document in which a clear and succinct statement of these rights can be most conveniently found. They were only discovered, not invented, by the founding fathers of this republic. Their development had a long prior history, and America has no monopoly on them.

It should be added that one citizen or group of citizens is not fully free in either secular or religious affairs if other citizens are unfairly favored to his disadvantage. A merchant or manufacturer may be free from governmental restraint in carrying on his business, but he is not really free to carry it on if the government subsidizes his competitors. Similarly, a church and its members may be free to worship, preach, teach, and publish, but they are not fully free to propagate their faith if the government lends support and official prestige to another church of differing faith.

The concept of religious liberty is relevant to union because only churches that are really free can be free to unite, and only individuals who are religiously free can be free to participate in a Church that is freely united. It should be carefully noted that the description of religious liberty as identical with civil liberty was specifically limited to liberty *as against either action or nonaction by the state.* There is another kind of liberty that is essential to unity. Much will be said about that later. It is the pivotal point in this book.

The second of the two ideas which were belated discoveries for me was that there have been two great revolutions in the history of the Church so far as concerns its own fundamental character and its relation to individuals and to the social order—or two great watersheds which divide the whole course of that history into three sections. The first of these watersheds was sharply marked, like the crest of a rugged mountain range; the second, like the continental divide at many places in the Southwest, was less conspicuous and abrupt, a more gradual alteration of the slope, but equally effective in changing the direction of the flow.

Before the first revolution the Church was a voluntary fellowship of persons who had become convinced of the saving power of Christ and the truth of his religion. Actually, the believers in Christ were not all in agreement, for there were many doctrinal differences, but the largest and most powerful group asserted that the Church was united in faith because it declared that those who held other views, the "heretics," were not in the Church at all. This was one way of having a doctrinally united Church—by casting out of it all who were not doctrinally united. But the orthodox Church, which had begun to call itself "Catholic," was still an entirely voluntary association composed of none but those who wanted to be in it.

Then came the first revolution, in the latter part of the fourth century. The effect of it was that orthodox "Catholic" Christianity became a compulsory religion for the entire Empire. The police power of the state was enlisted to compel the pagans to become Christian and the "heretics" to become "Catholic." So the Church got unity, at least west of the Adriatic. That unity continued, with some tensions and ruptures, for nearly 1,200 years. At the time of the Reformation the great Protestant churches adopted the same system within their several areas of dominance. This was the unity of compulsory conformity—unity without liberty.

The second revolution was the reversal of the first. It came gradually, late in the seventeenth century and still more in the eighteenth. The essence of it was the development of civil and, incidentally, of religious liberty. The result of it was the free nonconformist bodies in countries still having established churches and the denominational system in the United States.

But it was not liberty alone which produced division in the Church. It was liberty plus the idea that a standardized and

21

uniform pattern of thought and practice was essential to the unity of the Church and to the health and strength of every part of it. That idea had been cherished by practically all Christians beginning even earlier than the fourth century, and most of them cherish it still. When those compulsions were destroyed which alone had secured an approximate conformity to a single (Roman) pattern in Western Europe throughout the medieval period, then the Church split into several major divisions on both national and confessional lines, and each of these for a time maintained its solidarity as best it could by using the same instruments of compulsion, each within its own area. With the rise of civil and so of religious liberty in the Protestant countries—and ultimately in such a Catholic country as France, where there were effective rebellions against clericalism—nonconformists gained the legal right to exist and to propagate their faith. So were born the relatively free bodies of Dissenters. But these, in turn, still held, as Roman Catholicism and the Protestant state churches had held, that each must maintain uniformity of doctrine and ritual within itself. When the new civil liberty made Christians free to divide and the old insistence upon conformity to a pattern in each church compelled dissenters to separate, then the denominational system came to full flower.

Much more will be said about these two revolutions, the rise and fall of compulsory conformity or the total-population theory of the Church. They are the great turning points in the history of the unity of the Church.

Let us return now to the three items which were mentioned as indicating the scope and purpose of this discussion. The first of these—the exaltation of the ideal of a united Church—may almost be taken for granted. It is presupposed in all that follows. Few thoughtful readers will deny that unity is demanded:

by "God's design" for the Church;
by the will of Christ;
by the very concept of a Church;

by the work the Church has to do;

by the imperative principle of fellowship and "co.
   saints" among all professed followers of Christ.

Practically everyone knows this.

The conception of the Church as "essentially, inten   ..iy
and constitutionally one" is as old as the Church itself. It has
been held by most Christians throughout most of the nineteen
centuries of Christian history. Complacent sectarianism is a
thing of relatively recent origin, of limited geographical spread,
and of vanishing—now almost vanished—popularity. Because
of many attempted reforms that were only partly successful,
the Church became actually divided long before it occurred
to anyone to defend this shattered state by saying that it was
a fine thing for the Church to be divided. That opinion never
found elsewhere such wide acceptance as in the United States.
Many now living can remember the time when the majority of
American Christians took it for granted that sectarian division
was the normal and desirable state of the Church, and when it
was regarded as the mark of a liberal and tolerant mind to say
that it was a grand arrangement to have a large number of
different denominations so that everybody could find a church
that exactly suited his "temperament." I can well remember
some of the arguments in support of that view that I have
heard used in good faith and with deep earnestness even by
responsible religious leaders. It is unnecessary to repeat those
arguments now, for nobody now believes them. There are
many, of course, who consider the division of the Church into
many sects as unavoidable and irremediable, and it still remains to be proved that they are wrong. But few are now
willing to say that this condition is natural and right. To be
sure, some kinds of unity are worse than division, but that
does not mean that division is good.

Let us proceed, then, on the assumption that it is agreed
that the unity of the Church is a desirable, indeed an imperative,
objective.

The second part of our inquiry is concerned with history. It will involve outlining the history of the theory and practice of church unity in a few bold strokes, with the addition of some illustrative particulars and enough documentation from the sources to support the general statements that may be made. This will not be history for history's sake or merely for the satisfaction of an antiquarian curiosity as to what happened long ago. It will be history considered as throwing light on the contemporary situation and as affording some guidance in dealing with the problems that lie around us and ahead of us. What happened in the long ago cannot be ignored, for it conditions the present. This is especially true of such an institution as the Church, in relation to which the "sanction of history" is regarded by one school of thought as furnishing sufficient justification for existing structures and practices. The assurance that the Holy Spirit will "guide you into all truth" has had some unfortunate repercussions, or misapplications, chief of which is the facile assumption that every policy the Church has adopted or every idea that has been generally popular in it is something that the Holy Spirit has guided it into. But if the appeal is to history, then to history let us go.

The opposite type of mind, which is impatient of researches into history on the plea that they are mere evasions of present issues, may need to be reminded that present issues are defined by past events. If a man has what the doctors call "adhesions" resulting from an operation ten years ago, he cannot write them off as ancient history. The operation may be an old story—and perhaps one too often told—but the adhesions are a present fact. The Church in our day may be suffering seriously from adhesions which it acquired long ago. Or, to abandon the unsavory metaphor, it has carried over many ideas, habits, customs, and attitudes which it picked up in the course of its long history and which, whether or not they functioned legitimately and usefully then, need to be scrutinized critically to see whether they are helps or hindrances now. Part of that scrutiny must be an examination into their title to historical validity. The churches do not want to be caught defending a claim to stolen goods.

The historical aspect of our study, then, will lead us to consider such questions as these: What kind or kinds of unity has the Church tried to have, or actually had? By what institutions and practices did it try to establish and maintain its unity? What social and political principles were involved in its conceptions of unity and in the procedures that it adopted for the defense of its unity? What price did the Church, and humanity itself, pay for such unity as was attained? How did it work? If it failed, why and how did it fail? Under what conditions, if ever, has unity been worse than division? The answers to such questions should serve as buoys along the channel—they can warn us where *not* to sail on our voyage toward unity if we would avoid repeating the disasters of the past. This figure of speech gains fresh appropriateness with the recent adoption of the Church's ancient symbol—a ship bearing a cross—as the symbol of the World Council of Churches. The good ship *Oikumene* ought not to be steered upon reefs that can easily be charted from its earlier voyages.

The third main idea, as already stated, has to do with the conditions which must be regarded as "essential to the unity of the Church in the modern world." This obviously breaks into two parts: First, the nature of the Church; second, the nature of the modern world and the modern mind. The nature of the Church is a broad and deep subject which cannot here he discussed at the length which it invites and deserves. It will be sufficient for the present purpose to consider those aspects of it which bear most directly on its unity, and the related question as to how the indispensable characteristics of the Church are to be most reliably determined. In thinking of the nature of the modern world it will be necessary to note specifically those conceptions of human worth and freedom which modern man has won through a long process of trial and error, which he often uses foolishly, but which he will

25

never be foolish enough to surrender permanently, however seductively he may be tempted, cajoled, or exhorted.

As to the nature of the Church: I will start with the presupposition that the Church is a God-given thing. Whatever it is in its basic reality and essence, man did not originate it. This stipulation will probably be accepted by all who have any concern about the unity of the Church and therefore by all who would have any interest in reading this book. To say that the Church is God-given is to use a phrase that may be interpreted in various ways, ranging from legalistic to liberal. The author prefers to leave himself and the readers free within its generous boundaries. Of course it does not necessarily mean —and for this writer does not mean at all—that any particular feature of the historical Church must be regarded as of divine origin.

The objective and visible Church has had, and still has, many and diversified characteristics of belief and behavior. It has accumulated these in the course of its history. Every institution is molded and colored by the experiences through which it passes, by the cultural climate in which it lives, and by the ideas and desires of the men who are involved in it. The Church is no exception to this. We must resort to history and to observation of the contemporary scene to find answers to such questions as: How does the Church act? What does it look like? What are its patterns of thought and culture? What have been, and what are, its relations with other forms of human association and with the culture of any particular time and place? But if we ask, What *is* the Church in its fundamental and essential nature and in the divine intention? then I do not know of any reliable source of information other than the New Testament.

It is only fair to say that this last proposition is not undisputed. There are those who say that the New Testament gives only a somewhat sketchy picture of the *germ* of the Church, and that the actual nature of that God-given germ can be known only by observing what it developed into "under the guidance of the Holy Spirit"—assuming that the guidance of the Holy Spirit was the determining factor in the historic process of that development. By way of illustration it may be said that, if an apple seed were shown to even the most skilled botanist who had never before seen an apple seed, he could not possibly tell whether it was the seed of a tree, a vine, a shrub, or a flower. He could discover the essential nature and, so to speak, the divine intention of that seed only by planting it and seeing what it grows into. The analogy is attractive, but it is false, as so many attractive analogies are. The two kinds of growth that are being compared are not comparable. Biological and social growth are entirely distinct processes. Soil, climate, and care determine *how* the appleseed shall grow but not *what* it shall grow into. No human manipulation can bring out of it a strawberry plant or an oak tree. But a social institution can be radically transformed. Given plenty of time and the operation of human motives and social forces, there can be a complete transformation of its character, purpose, procedure, and structure, all so gradually carried out that a certain institutional continuity is preserved. The resulting institution may be better or worse than the original, but the one certain thing about the whole process is that no one could determine the nature of the original by observing what has "developed"out of it; for, as a matter of fact, the characteristics of the resulting structure are not developments from the original but are features superimposed upon it or substituted for it.

In seeking the essential nature of the Church then, I repeat, the important thing is to try to find what it was when it began. Little light is thrown on that by considering what it became in a dying and disintegrating Roman Empire, or in a Europe awakened by the Renaissance and the Reformation, or in denominationalized America. The only recourse is to the New Testament. Even there we shall not find the Church unaffected by its cultural environment and by the pressure of social forces, but we can come closer to understanding what God meant the Church to be than by reliance upon other sources.

All this does not imply that the Church is necessarily bound to every pattern of procedure and organization that was practiced by the New Testament churches. Changing situations require changed methods. Some further consideration will need to be given later to that point. At present we are considering the Church's *nature,* not its methods. But even here it may be well to note an important distinction between two things that are easily confused: first, the *right and freedom* of the Church to adopt new methods and processes for the efficient accomplishment of its mission; and second, the *power and authority* of the Church, if any, to make the acceptance of its new procedures and structures mandatory upon all Christians, to the prejudice of their rights and freedom.

The point is sometimes made that the Church must be a more basic authority than the New Testament, even for defining the nature of the Church, because the "Church produced the New Testament." It is of course true in a certain limited sense that the Church did produce the New Testament. The writings were produced within the Church (not by it), and the Church decided which writings should be included in the canon of Christian Scripture. The community of Christians did this in a slow, gradual, and somewhat informal way by the growth of a consensus. Only after about three hundred years did this consensus become virtually unanimous for all the books of the New Testament. (It is not yet unanimous for the Old Testament, for Roman Catholics accept as part of it those writings which Protestants generally omit from the canon and call "Apocrypha.")

The growth of the New Testament canon is an interesting and important story the details of which have no place here. But though it took long to complete the canon and come to agreement about it, it must be remembered that, from the time when it began to be agreed that *some* Christian writings should be regarded as "Scripture" (and that was about A.D.

28

175), there was never a moment's doubt as to the valid claim of about nine tenths of our New Testament to a place in that category. The disputes concerned only a few books of questionable authorship, such as Hebrews, Revelation, and II Peter, and the inclusion of some dubious Gospels which were ultimately rejected on the ground that they were postapostolic and that they contained too large an infusion of unreliable legend. The process of literary and historical criticism (that is, "higher criticism") began as early as that! The main decisions about the contents of the New Testament canon were made by the common consent of common Christians and, still more, by the gradually harmonizing practice of local churches in the selection of books sufficiently edifying to be read in public services of worship. These main decisions were made long before the Church as a whole had any sort of central organizations, or even any regional organizations, that could profess to act with authority on this or any other subject. Only with these important limitations can it be said that the "Church produced the New Testament." It is truer to the facts to say that the Christian movement and the Christian community produced the New Testament at the same time that they were producing Church organization in a cohesive and somewhat authoritative form—and that the first of these processes (producing the New Testament) was considerably more rapid than the latter.

It is, of course, obviously true that the Church as described in the New Testament is older than the New Testament— even older than any of the separate writings contained in it. Otherwise the New Testament could not be, as it is, our source of information about the origin and nature of the Church. To that source we must go, and by its testimony we must abide, if we want reliable information concerning the original character and essential nature of the Church.

This is absolutely basic to any definition of the conditions which are "essential to the unity of the Church in the modern world." Christians in the modern world will not unite in any ecumenical Church which does not preserve the essential character of the New Testament Church as they understand it. To be sure, millions are now members of churches which have little visible resemblance to the Church as depicted in the New Testament. Even these justify their position by holding that the New Testament gives warrant for believing that the Church had within itself from the beginning such a power of "development" that its later authoritative creeds and authoritarian policies are validated by the historical process which produced them. But a merger of many sects on that basis would result only in a larger sect which, however impressive its size and however great its social and political prestige, would still not be a united Church. For there are still other millions whose interest in union among the professed followers of Christ cannot be enlisted in support of any program for unity which does not embody the essential characteristics that they think they find in the early Church as portrayed in the New Testament, or which is based on the hypothesis that whatever the Church develops out of that "germ" is authentic and binding.

This same question, as to the conditions of a united Church in the modern world, must also be approached from the other side, by considering the mind of the modern world. Modern man is much more keenly aware of his rights and more insistent upon his liberties than men generally were in earlier ages. Christianity is one of the principal forces that have made him so. Love of liberty and determination to have it do not, to be sure, represent a new attitude, but their wide prevalence is new. It is rooted in the Christian conception of the worth and dignity of man and is in harmony with the New Testament's representation of Christianity and of the Church. Modern Christian men believe that God means man to be free. They are not satisfied with the fatally qualified dictum that *"true* freedom" is "freedom to do what is right and to believe and speak what is true"—with the accompanying presupposition that some select and self-perpetuating group has the authority to define the right and the true. The modern Christian man's demand for liberty for himself and others on the ground that they are children of God is supported by considerations of a more secular nature and finds expression also in secular areas. In this connection the terms "modern" and "secular" are used with none of the odium which is often associated with them. Modern man—including modern Christian man—will not sacrifice his God-given and blood-bought liberty. Fidelity to its Master demands that the Church shall be equally concerned. If the championing of human freedom is not a condition of the Church's survival, it is certainly a condition of its unity.

Therefore, one condition of a just and durable unity that needs to be heavily stressed is *liberty*—the freedom of the Church itself from domination by secular forces, whether governmental, sociological, or cultural, and the freedom of the Christian man from both secular and ecclesiastical tyranny. Religious liberty thus includes the freedom *of* the Church and the freedom of individuals in relation to religion. The religious liberty of individuals includes the freedom of all men from interference by the state in the area of their faith and worship, and the freedom of Christians *in* the Church.

These two aspects of religious liberty, the institutional and the individual, are quite distinct from each other. The first (freedom *of* the Church) can exist without the second. The second, in so far as it relates to Christians, can scarcely exist without the first. Indeed, the first of these kinds of freedom (freedom of the Church from external control) has existed, subject to some important limitations, throughout the greater part of the history of Christendom, at least west of the Adriatic. In fact, it was the only kind that did exist for a good deal more than a thousand years. In some places it is still virtually the only kind of religious freedom that exists.

This freedom *of* the Church has often been abused *by* the Church. At times the Church has developed and exploited the idea that it would not have its essential freedom to "carry out

31

its spiritual mission" unless it had the freedom and the power to override all other freedoms, to reduce all human institutions to the status of its subordinate agents, and to hold all men as its obedient subjects.

I need not say how radically I resent and reject such usurpation. Nevertheless, the Church must be free. No phase of its life in the modern world can be discussed without that presupposition. Certainly its unity cannot be profitably discussed on any other terms. It is therefore useless to talk about a united and ecumenical Church which will include within itself those churches which complacently accept rigid control by secular governments or those which permit themselves to be used as instruments of governmental policy by the rulers of the state. Only pathetic and futile (however sincere) gestures toward unity can be made by churches so hampered by the secular power that they cannot publicly proclaim and propagate their faith, cannot freely select and educate their own ministry, or cannot engage in Christian social service, or are so restricted that they are driven into the back streets and forced to lead a quasi-catacomb existence. Still more disqualified for fruitful ecumenical conversation is any church which allies itself with government to suppress or hamper the other churches in its area.

In this connection it must be frankly recognized that a special difficulty exists when it comes to defining realistically a unity which would include both established and "free" churches. It must not be said that the difficulty is insuperable, but it exists, and this in spite of the very great liberalization of the practices of the Protestant established churches in northern Europe and the British Isles and the governments with which they are associated. It is my opinion, after many years of participation in the work of ecumenical conferences, commissions, and committees, that one of the serious road blocks on the way toward unity is the divergence in concepts of the Church held by representatives of these two types of churches. The backgrounds and bases of these two concepts will be indicated in the historical chapters that are to follow.

Churches need to be free in order to live the normal life of churches, to bear the responsibilities that rest upon them as churches, to do the things that it is the business of churches to do, to maintain their testimony separately if they believe this to be their duty, and to unite freely with other churches if in their judgment this is a step toward realizing God's design for the visible manifestation of a united Church. But churches do not need any grant or confirmation of special privileges or liberties by the state based upon the state's recognition that the Church is a unique and divinely authorized form of association. This is, of course, the precise opposite of the Roman Catholic doctrine—clearly and emphatically expressed in Pope Leo XIII's great encyclical *Immortale Dei,* "On the Christian Constitution of States"—which holds that it is outrageous and disastrous for a state not to treat the Roman Catholic Church as a unique and divinely authorized institution havings rights and powers possessed by no other organization, secular or religious. The point cannot be argued at length. It should be noted, however, that the pope's claim to special rights and immunities for the Church as such involves no inconsistency because it is accompanied by a thoroughgoing repudation of the principle of religious liberty for individuals.

It is sufficient for our purpose to put the two positions side by side so that the contrast between them may be clear. The pope's position is: (1) that religious liberty for individuals is a ruinous evil that grew out of the "harmful and lamentable rage for innovation which rose to a climax in the 16th century," and that it ought to be done away with; and (2) that the Church has inherent rights and liberties of a unique sort that are independent of any rights which its members may possess as men, and that what is now needed is for the social order to return to the happy condition that existed before the sixteenth century when the Roman Catholic Church "established firmly in befitting dignity, flourished everywhere by the favor of princes and the legitimate protection of magistrates." The view presented in this book is: (1) that religious liberty for individuals is an inseparable aspect of civil liberty and is as inalienable as the rights of life, liberty of the person, and pursuit of happiness; and (2) that the guarantee of civil and religious liberty to individuals inevitably guarantees to the Church and to all the churches all the liberty they need and the free exercise of all the rights they legitimately have.

When the Church was free to exercise the rights that the pope claims for it, it was free to exercise its power and to invoke the power of the state to enforce the unity of "submission to Rome," thereby suppressing all other liberties that might conflict with this program of compulsory unity and conformity. That unity broke down. It failed because the Roman Catholic Church had the wrong definition of the Church's rights and liberties. The Church still needs to be free if it is to be strong and united, and meanwhile all the churches must be free. But this freedom must be a freedom which rests upon the rights and liberties of free men, not one that supresses them.

There is no place in this book for any "anti-Catholic" tirade, but it is well to understand at the outset that I have no interest in any program for a united Church unified under a central authority, at Rome or elsewhere, which determines the patterns of faith and worship which all men must follow and utilizes the police power of the state, when it can command it, to suppress dissent.

Not only must the Church and the churches be free, but the individual Christians within these churches must also be free. As already suggested, this individual freedom is of two kinds. The first is freedom from pressure by the civil power to enforce conformity to a favored church and, conversely, freedom from civil disabilities as a penalty for nonconformity. That is what is meant by the familiar words "freedom to worship God according to the dictates of conscience." There is really a good deal more to it than that, though that is the first great essential. At the least this means assurance that one will not be hanged by the neck or put in jail for going to the wrong church or to none, or be fined and imprisoned for "preaching without a license," or be deprived of the rights of citizenship or made ineligible for public office because one lacks the proper ecclesiastical connection. Do these seem such obvious demands of simple justice that no one could ever think of denying them? The sad truth is that in the total course of Christian history all of them have been much more generally denied than granted. Freedom of dissent from an established religion and freedom from civil penalties for such dissent are still enjoyed only under severe limitations in large areas of what is called Christendom. Where religious liberty for individuals is denied by Christian states, this almost invariably has been done and is done by the connivance and at the insistence of a dominant and favored church. And it may be observed that this kind of religious liberty is exactly the kind for which all Christians pled and in advocacy of which some of the greatest early Christians wrote during the early centuries of Christianity in the Roman Empire when the old pagan religion was still in the saddle.

In spite of what may be true in backward areas, this kind of religious liberty very generally exists in the modern world. For our present purpose the exceptions may be ignored, and it may be hoped that in so far as religious liberty as against repressive action by the state has not been completely attained, the increasing respect for the fundamental human rights and recognition of civil liberties will take care of that matter in the not too distant future.

The other kind of religious liberty for individuals is freedom not from but *within* the church. This is the important contemporary problem, so far as unity within the orbit of Protestantism is concerned. This point should be printed in red ink. Everything else hinges on it. All the rest of this book will bear, directly or indirectly, on the proposition that a united Church may possibly be attained if freedom within the Church can be attained, and that it cannot possibly be attained otherwise.

But I hasten to add, lest the problem seem to be oversimplified, that, while freedom both in the state and in the Church is a condition which is essential to any just and durable unity, freedom is not in itself a unifying principle. We shall have to consider also what Christians are going to do with their freedom when they get it. Liberty means an open field for thought and action. The unifying force must be looked for not in the mere openness of the field, but in the quality of the thinking and acting that take place in it. Nevertheless, the openness of the field is a prime essential, and it therefore demands primary consideration—especially because the great weight of Christian tradition is against it.

Those who make much of the "witness of history" for the validation of Christian institutions must make what apology they can for the fact that thorughout by far the greater part of its history the Church has been a persecuting Church. When it has not been preserving its unity by threats and violence, its divided sects have been preserving their purity as well as their separate unities by the exclusion of all who did not conform to their respective standards. The only large exceptions to this sweeping generalization are the brief period at the beginning before the excommunication of "heretics" became standard practice, a few relatively small communions in recent times, and the fact that in these days laymen are seldom excluded for private heresy. Apart from these exceptions the individual Christian man has never simultaneously enjoyed freedom from governmental pressures and restraints on his religion, and liberty of thought and conscience within an organized church; and generally he has had neither. The history of religious liberty is largely the history of its denial. The disciplined and willing conformist, the completely indifferent conformist, and the conscientious and convinced conformist, of course, are not unpleasantly affected by the lack of liberty.

We turn now to certain aspects of history which are directly relevant to the unity of the Church.

Chapter II

The Early Church

NOT DIVIDED, BUT NOT YET UNITED

BEFORE CONSIDERING THE FIRST REVOLUTION, WHICH WAS THE pivotal point between the early Church and the medieval Church—the revolution which Constantine initiated, which Theodosius may be said (though not quite so positively) to have completed, and for which St. Augustine served as god-father, advocate, and theological interpreter—it will be necessary to give some attention to the Church of the first three centuries, but only to those features of it which have an evident relation to its unity. Even with this limitation there are important points upon which the judgment of scholars is not unanimous. My intention is to present as factual material only those things upon which there is general agreement among the well informed, and to make it clearly evident when I am stating what I believe to be the consensus of reputable scholarship and when I am offering opinions or interpretations which, whether correct or not, are disputable.

At the outset, and in view of the contrasting situation that was to develop later, it must be noted that membership in the Church was voluntary. This may seem too obvious to require mention. It is indeed so obvious that it is seldom mentioned in the most learned discussions of the "essential nature" of the Church, yet it is a fact of the most radical importance. Christians were Christian by conviction, not compulsion. The Church was made up of such Christians. If, as in all forms of voluntary association, there were some whose conviction did not go very deep—some, for example, who responded to family pressure, or fell in love with a Christian girl, or followed the influence of some admired Christian leader without knowing what made him admirable—still, the character of the Church as a voluntary association was not thereby compromised. It was much more than that, but it was *that*. The Church, as we have agreed, was created not by the will of man but by the act of God, but no man became a member of it without his own consent freely given. To forget or obscure that fact in the interest of exalting the Church as a more-than-human institution is to omit an essential element in defining the "nature of the Church." The New Testament Church had no members who did not want to be members of it.

I linger upon the point, obvious and indisputable as it is, because so many scholars seem determined to overlook or underrate it or to pervert the meaning of it. I have asserted in a company of able theologians that "membership in the Church of the first century was purely voluntary," only to have them rise in alarm and shout in chorus, "What! Do you mean to say that the Church came into existence by the will of man?" "No, brethren," I would respond. "The Church did not come into existence by the will of man. It came into existence by the determinate purpose of God. But it does appear, from the way in which Peter and Paul preached, that God left to every man the decision as to whether he would become a member of that Church." At this juncture some theological discussion about predestination and effectual calling would be inevitable, but irrelevant, for the point is that those who accepted the gospel and became members of the Church, under whatever promptings of the divine Spirit, still made their decision and took the action by their own will and under no compulsion by either civil or ecclesiastical authorities. The choice was theirs. The Church was made up of those who freely chose to be in the Church. This was true in the first century. It was not true at the end of the fourth. This contrast is the most important difference between these two periods for the purpose of our present study of the unity of the Church. To overlook this contrast is to miss everything. Therefore I say again: The Church of the first century was a Church with a voluntary membership.

In studying the early Church one must distinguish between the Church as it was in the apostolic age (approximately the first century) and the Church as it was in the second and third centuries. For the first of these periods the source of information is the New Testament; for the second, the writings of the post-apostolic and ante-Nicene Fathers, supplemented by the scanty references in secular history. The following chapter will deal with the second and third centuries and part of the fourth.

It is in vain that one would look in the New Testament for any explicit statement as to when the Church came into existence, or any rules laid down for its procedure, or any pattern authoritatively prescribed for its organization. Whether it began with the call of Abraham (as I do not believe and may later have occasion to try to disprove) or when Jesus called his first disciples (as P. T. Forsyth in his *The Principle of Authority* argues that it did, if not earlier) or on the day of Pentecost when Peter preached the first gospel sermon and won the first converts to it, certainly the Church did not begin by being organized. It did not start with a constitution and by-laws. To say that the Church *was,* or *is,* an organization is to misrepresent and belittle it. The Church existed before it had any organization. Of the two mentions of it that are ascribed to Jesus (Matt. 16:18 and 18:17), one definitely locates its beginning in the future ("I *will* build"), the other seems clearly anticipatory, and neither gives any hint as to its organization or structure. The words of Matt. 18:17—"tell it unto the church" and the instructions as to what to do if an offender will not "hear the church"—suggest a compact and harmonious local company that might be expected to act by consensus, like a Quaker meeting, but give no hint of official leadership or of authoritative voices within it. This may reflect the state of the Church about the years 70 to 80 when the Gospel of Matthew was probably written, or earlier, when the materials which entered into that Gospel were taking form.

The references to the Church in Acts and the Epistles assume its existence, give some hints as to its actual structure locally in various cities, and frequently and emphatically assert the spiritual unity of the Church as a fellowship of believers who are one in Christ; but they present no indication whatever of any unifying organization for the Church as a whole. I am willing to take as my own the words of W. O. Carver in his *The Glory of God in the Christian Calling:*

However one may interpret the fact in its significance for Christian history, it is a fact that in the New Testament there is no one general organized Christian body—no one visible institution of which the visible local bodies are member units. These local units are responsible to and under the administrative guidance of no central individual or group of any sort, anywhere. The local bodies are fellowships rather than institutions or branches of an institution. Their officers are functional rather than institutional. All Christians ("saints") are encouraged and earnestly exhorted to cultivate a sense of unity with and a unique "love for all the saints." The Christian movement is one Church, but the churches are not under nor in one church in any outward, institutional sense.[1]

Yet it is indisputable that even the earliest Christians thought of the Church as constituting a whole. Though the phrase "One Lord, one faith, one baptism" (Eph. 4:5) was coined fairly late in the apostolic age, it says nothing that could not have been said in the first decade of the Church's life, though in either case "faith" must be given a very simple meaning. Fellowship in faith and in devotion to one Lord bound Christians together in little groups of "two or three" (Matt. 18:20) and also bound these groups together into a total unity which

[1] (Nashville, Tenn.: Broadman Press, 1949), p. 56. Used by permission of the Sunday School Board of the Southern Baptist Convention.

was so real that Paul could call it the "body of Christ," or a body of which Christ is the head, or a building of which he is the cornerstone. There must naturally have been a considerable difference between the ideas expressed by an apostle in teaching new converts and inexperienced Christians, and the ideas generally held by such Christians. Nevertheless, there is no reason to doubt that as soon as these learned anything about the religion which they were adopting, or were about to adopt, or had recently adopted, they learned that the acceptance of Christ involved entering the fellowship of all those who had accepted him, and that the "body" formed by this fellowship with him and with one another *was* the Church. This body was the *Corpus Christi*. The idea of a *Corpus Christianum,* a Christian community or nation including its entire population regardless of their personal faith or character, came much later and has no New Testament authority.

To say that the Church had existence, vitality, and a sense of its own unity before it had organization is not to say that organization is unimportant for the continuing life and work of the Church. Nor is it to say that there were no "authorities" the acknowledgment of which by the earliest Christians was essential to their cohesion in Christian fellowship. We shall come presently to a consideration of these authorities and of the ways in which some of them gave place to authorities of a different kind.

The unity of the Church in the apostolic age may be approached by considering three aspects of its life: the *fellowship* which it practiced, the *faith* which it professed, and the *authorities* which it recognized. The order in which these items are mentioned is the reverse of the order of causation: Christians had fellowship because they had a common faith, and they had this faith because they had received it from what may be called "authorities," if the term is taken in a broad enough sense. But the order in which they are mentioned, and will be briefly described, is that in which they would have been seen by an observer.

41

Fellowship was certainly the most noticeable characteristic of the early disciples. Theirs was a life together. As Jesus and his little group of intimate followers had a common purse from which the wants of all were supplied, so the members of the first Christian community, in Jerusalem, for a time "had all things common," and none of them said "that ought of the things which he possessed was his own." This community of property was neither complete, compulsory, nor permanent, nor was the practice followed, even so far as it was followed, because of any theory about the sinfulness of holding property but because, like members of a good family, they were deeply concerned for one another's welfare. (It may be remarked parenthetically that, since this experiment in "Christian communism" was never meant to include any who were not Christians and was purely voluntary even for them, it does not even point in the direction of giving Christian sanction to a communist social order for general and compulsory application in a mixed society of Christians and non-Christians.) But even though the practice of the common purse and the common table was not long continued and probably did not extend outside Jerusalem, it exhibited conspicuously that sense of total brotherhood which bound Christians together in intimate groups even where this particular system was never adopted. These little companies of believers not only were what the sociologists call free-to-face groups; they were also hand-in-hand and heart-to-heart groups. The frequency with which the apostles, following the very words of Jesus as well as his spirit, exhorted them to "love one another" may suggest—what one would in any case suppose—that the practice of Christians in this respect did not always perfectly correspond with the ideal; but it testifies also to the urgency which the responsible leaders attached to this aspect of the Church's life.

As Christians found themselves increasingly cut off from association with their former friends, they were driven as well as drawn into closer comradeship with one another, as missionaries and native Christians are today in non-Christian countries.

With the rise of Christian communities in widely scattered places the range of this fellowship increased. Peter's enlightening experience with Cornelius and Paul's amazing exploits of travel and evangelism in Asia Minor, Greece, and Italy complicated the problem of fellowship by introducing racial, cultural, and social variety into the household of faith, and there is evidence (though not in the New Testament) that the missionary work of other apostles in lands east of Judea brought into the Church other elements which did not easily coalesce with those in the west. But within the limits imposed by distance, the difficulties of travel and communication, differences of culture and language (in spite of the wide spread of *koine* Greek), and the natural human tendency to concentrate on local interests, Christians of the apostolic age had a sense of participation in a new order which included all of them. This conception became, in effect, a part of that gospel to which they were converted. Paul was "sent" on his first missionary journey by the church at Antioch, even though the record does not show that it gave him anything but its blessing. He acknowledges financial and other help from the brethren at Philippi. He took a collection in Greece for the "poor saints which are at Jerusalem." Traveling evangelists—we know only a few of them by name, but there must have been many more in view of the rapid multiplication of churches in Asia Minor, Greece, Italy, and elsewhere—proved the existence of a bond of common interest which knit the scattered believers into one Church.

It is reckless to say—as has been said by some—that the way to salvation through Christ was never presented except as salvation in, through, and by the Church, and that the idea of "individual salvation" never entered anyone's mind. There are too many recorded cases of conversion in which personal salvation was precisely the point of emphasis and in which there is no mention of the Church, either explicitly or implicitly (for example, Pentecost, Acts 2; the Ethiopian, Acts 8:35-39; Cornelius, Acts 10; Antioch, Acts 11:20, 21; Antioch in Pisidia,

43

Acts 13:47, 48; the jailor at Philippi, Acts 16:30, 31). But this exaggeration does not invalidate the general truth which it is injudiciously designed to support—namely, that converts *did* enter a local fellowship if one were available or constitute one if there were enough of them, and that they became quickly, if not always immediately, aware of their participation in a universal fellowship which embraced all believers, and aware too that participation in this fellowship was integral with the gospel which they had accepted.

It is unfortunate that we do not have more documentary evidence as to what the ordinary first-century Christians actually thought and did. The book of Acts and the epistles tell what some of the leaders did and what these leaders, especially Paul, said that Christians ought to think and do. To be sure, some of Paul's letters, especially to the church at Corinth, reveal clearly enough some of the shortcomings and transgressions of members of that church. The doctrinal and even the moral instructions which have been preserved indicate patterns of belief and behavior which the apostles held before Christians as objectives for their attainment or as authoritative guides for their thought and action. It is clear from these instructions that there were some departures from the faith (for example, denial "that Jesus Christ is come in the flesh," II John 7) and some pagan sins (Rom. 1) which were regarded as so deadly that they would automatically destroy the possibility of Christian fellowship. But the bulk of these precepts, earnest and authoritative as they are, are not presented as establishing criteria for either entering or continuing in that fellowship which was the Church. It was not a society of those who behaved perfectly and thought correctly about the mysteries of the faith, but a comprehensive fellowship of all who professed to be followers of Jesus Christ.

That ideal and spiritual oneness of all Christians probably could not long have survived without concrete expression. Local churches expressed their unity by intimate association, by meetings for worship, by the observance of the Lord's Supper, and by mutual aid. Christian communities in widely separated places manifested and cultivated the larger unity by letters, by gifts (as for the poor saints at Jerusalem), by visits and migrations, and by the exercise of hospitality. A brother was a brother, wherever he might go, and there was much travel in the Roman Empire. Some were inclined to abuse the hospitality offered by the brethren and their care for the local poor, and to loaf at their expense, for Paul administered a warning about this in the first letter he ever wrote to a church (I Thess. 4:11), but with so little effect that he had to repeat it more emphatically in his second letter to the same church (II Thess. 3:10, "If any would not work, neither should he eat"). That this abuse continued in spite of warnings proves that the practice of hospitality also continued. Traveling teachers and evangelists, even after Paul's time, did much to knit together the separated communities; but some of these were imposters. The Didache (about A.D. 100) lays down a simple rule for detecting them:

Let every apostle who comes to you be welcomed as the Lord. But he shall not stay more than one day, and if it is necessary, the next day also. But if he stays three days, he is a false prophet. And when an apostle leaves, let him take nothing except bread to last until he finds his next lodging. But if he asks for money, he is a false prophet. (11:4-6.) [2]

Practical fellowship in either evangelistic or charitable works beyond the local circle was limited by the lack of any agencies of co-operation and still more by the absence of any definite objectives for united action. It was unlikely that the Church could have any practical program for achievement in this present world so long as its dominant mood was that of waiting for the end of the age, the coming of Christ in apocalyptic splendor, and the dawning of a new era. The Church's interest

[2] From *The Apostolic Fathers: An American Translation,* by Edgar J. Goodspeed (New York: Harper & Bros., 1950), p. 16.

was more eschatological than missionary. Jesus had told his disciples to "go" into all the world, and many of them went far and preached widely. But neither he nor the apostles told the churches to "send." (Paul's "How shall they preach, except they be sent?" [Rom. 10:15] had no context of appeal to the Church to do anything.) The early Church had some great missionaries, including the greatest one that ever lived, but there is no evidence that the church, either generally or locally, felt any great responsibility for forwarding the missionary enterprise. Philippi was virtually unique in its aid to Paul.

But in spite of the limitations imposed by the absence of any recognized common task, and in spite of such hindrances as racial prejudice, cultural diversity, class distinctions, local preoccupation, and the difficulties of travel and communication, the Church of the first century achieved in a remarkable degree the sense of being a universal fellowship embracing all believers in Christ. Such brotherhood was a new thing upon earth, and it was marvelous alike in the eyes of believers and unbelievers. It was one of the major miracles attending the origin of our religion.

If fellowship was the attitude which Christians manifested to one another and a phenomenon which the world could see, the ground of it was their common *faith*. This faith was an undefined but wholehearted trust in one Lord, accompanied by a desire to do his will, a belief that he had in a very real sense come from God, that he had been a man in the flesh, had been crucified and had risen and gone back to God, and a vivid hope of his imminent return to earth and of eternal life through him. This faith was not embodied in a creed or definite formulation of doctrine, either written or unwritten. It is not recorded that any other profession of faith was required of penitent converts than that they "be baptized . . . in the name of Jesus Christ" (Acts 2:38) or declare, "I believe that Jesus Christ is the Son of God" (Acts 8:37) or "believe on the Lord Jesus Christ" (Acts 16:31). W. R. Matthews, dean of St. Paul's in London, says he regards it as the greatest calamity in the history of the Church that it ever adopted any other criterion of faith than the original one, which was "Jesus is Lord."

The extent to which the saving power of Jesus Christ was presented and accepted as related to the course of God's dealings with ancient Israel, seems to have varied according to the circumstances—as it naturally would, since on some occasions it was announced to Jews who had an intimate knowledge of that history and on other occasions to Gentiles who knew nothing about it. Peter's Pentecost sermon at Jerusalem (which of course was addressed to Jews) stressed the status of Jesus, a "man approved of God," as a descendant of David and the heir to his throne, and as one who had been foretold by the prophets, crucified by the very persons whom he was then addressing, raised and exalted by the right hand of God, and "made . . . both Lord and Christ." Philip began with the passage in Isaiah which the Ethiopian was reading and "preached unto him Jesus," but whether he went backward as well as forward from that text and how much more he derived from prophecy than a foretelling of the meek spirit in which Jesus received his death sentence, the record does not say. In any case, the Ethiopian was doubtless a Jewish proselyte and a keeper of the law. In the brief accounts of Paul's many sermons that led to conversions, much is left to the imagination, and there is little evidence as to the extent to which he developed the Hebrew background of the mission of Jesus. The point of our inquiry here, of course, is not what that background really was but how much the early Gentile converts knew about it or were expected to know.

Writing to the partly Jewish church at Rome, Paul exalts the example of Abraham because he was a man of faith, and quotes David as ascribing more blessedness to the man who trusts God for forgiveness than to him who relies on his own righteousness; but the redeeming work of Christ is regarded as the antithesis, rather than the corollary, of everything else in the religious regime of Israel. Earlier, in writing to the

Galatians to warn them against "Judaizers," Paul had even more pointedly rejected the idea of any continuity through the Hebrew nation and the religion of Israel to the Christian regime. There were, he said, two lines of descent from Abraham. One was through Isaac and Moses and the people of Israel, who were under the Law. That ends in failure because no man can be justified under the law. The other line, having no visible or racial continuity with Abraham (for nothing significant comes from the descendants of Ishmael), nevertheless is the true inheritor of the covenant which God made with Abraham as a man of faith. Sinai "gendereth to bondage," but "Christ hath made us free." In other words, those who have faith in God as Abraham had faith in God are the true heirs to the promise made to Abraham. The bodily descendants of Abraham through his grandson Jacob (or Israel) have forfeited their heritage by their unbelief and disobedience. Paul sees the Christians of his day not as a "new Israel" carrying on the line of the old Israel, but as a company of believers who had become the spiritual sons of Abraham because they had a faith like his. Israel had had its chance and failed. Christians were a new "people of God," not a "new Israel." Later, in Ephesians, the apostle strikes a still loftier note in declaring that Christ has "broken down the middle wall of partition" between Jews and Gentiles by bringing the Gentiles under the covenant of promise through faith and at the same time freeing the Jews by abolishing the "law of commandments contained in ordinances," so that they too in spite of their previous failure could be of the people of God on new terms.

I do not have the boldness to maintain that this one-paragraph sketch of a theme on which more learned men have written large volumes is infallibly correct, even within the limits of its brevity, though it represents my best judgment in the light of the available data. But this, at least, seems indisputably clear—that faith in Jesus Christ, as the rank and file of first-century Christians held it, could not have included universal agreement upon any elaborated doctrine concerning the relation of Jesus to Abraham, Moses, and David, or the relation of the Christian Church to the religious institutions of Israel. This was no part of the "faith."

It should be added that Jewish Christians retained, and Gentile Christians soon acquired, a reverence for the Hebrew sacred books as in a unique sense Holy Scripture. Writings which were to constitute the New Testament were revered, but it was long before they were regarded as in that category. The Old Testament was the Bible (though this inclusive term came later) of the early Church, and it never ceased to be a part of the Church's Bible. Marcion, who rejected it, was the first formidable heretic. Christian scholars studied profoundly the sacred history from creation to the Exile, often giving it fantastic allegorical interpretations to make it more serviceable to Christian piety, and the prophets proved to be a permanent and indispensable resource for both devotions and apologetics. But all this was no part of that essential common faith which gave to the Church of the first century its fellowship and unity.

Similarly, the elaborated Christological and trinitarian formulas of the fourth-century creeds and the systems of theology embodied in the great Reformation confessions go far beyond anything that the first Christians were expected to affirm or could have been expected to understand. That any or all of these venerable documents may give only systematic statements of truths that are to be found in the Scriptures is not here disputed. But there are many scriptural statements which were not test questions for admission to Christian fellowship or retention in it. The body of Paul's doctrinal teaching—for example, about justification and the atonement in Romans— was certainly in no sense the creed of the Church either as a test for admission or as the common belief of the members. Paul doubtless wrote it because, while he considered these doctrines true and important, he knew that Christians generally did not hold them.

Above all, the faith was Christ-centered. One might say that

49

the faith *was* Christ. To believe that Jesus was Christ, Lord, Savior, and to put one's trust in him and try to do his will— that was to have faith. To have such faith, it was necessary to know that Christ had lived, taught, and died and was alive. To trust in him, it was necessary to believe that he was real and that his relation to God the Father was so intimate that it could be best described by saying that he was God's Son. To do his will, it was necessary to know something about his teachings. The teachers and members of the Church were the custodians of the oral tradition of the teachings of Jesus. Their memories held all that was known and all that could ever be known of his words. No written records of them were in circulation for many years, so far as we know, but doubtless some collections of his sayings were being made and some memoranda of the story of his life. Some of these teachers, especially the apostles, and some of the members had seen and heard him. Most of them had heard the voices of those who had seen and heard him. They knew about his life and death, and the witnesses of his resurrection were among them. Jesus was to them no distant or legendary figure, no character in a book. He was a real and recent personality, a loved and living Lord, a redeemer mighty to save.

Differences of opinion about many matters in the realm of doctrine began to spring up very early. There were divergent views about the relation of Christianity to Judaism, about the importance of Jewish ceremonial, about the relation of grace to law. These grew partly out of differences of religious inheritance and cultural background. Ways were found of avoiding division on the ground of these differences, but more threatening were the beginnings of personal partisanships, which Paul rebuked sharply.

There was, of course, no New Testament to which appeal could be made, and no doctrine of infallibility residing in any man or group of men or characterizing any writing or collection of writings representing Christianity. There is no evidence that Christians believed or were expected to believe that the apostles were inerrant either in their oral teachings or in their writings. Yet the Christian movement, the Church, was not without effective leadership which had all the authority it needed.

What, then, were the *authorities* upon which the early Church received and held the *faith* which was the ground of its *fellowship* and so of its unity?

The concept of "authority" is not a simple one, and the word is not free from ambiguity. There is the authority which is derived from office in an orderly and organized society—the right to command accompanied by the power to enforce obedience or inflict a penalty for disobedience. This is the authority of the policeman or of the judge. One does not have to love these wielders of authority; one does not even have to think that their decisions are right or their actions just; one simply has to obey their lawful orders or take the unpleasant consequences. Then there is the authority of the expert, the man who knows. One trusts the pilot, not because he is infallibly right, but because he is more likely to be right than the passenger. He has made it his business to know the channel, and his skill has been certified by those who have made it their business to test the competence of pilots. Or one gives weight to the testimony of an eyewitness because he is in a position to know the facts better than those who did not see the event. This reduces to the authority of truth, but truth must always be mediated either through one's own apprehension of it or through agents or agencies which there is reason to accept as more reliable than one's own independent processes of understanding. Finally there is "moral authority"—a term that itself needs more thorough analysis than can be given to it here. This is the least dependent upon office or status, makes the greatest demand for inner acceptance rather than mere outward conformity or passive acquiescence, and states its imperative in terms of "ought" rather than "must."

The authority of God and of Christ includes some measure of all three kinds. It appears that all three elements can be found in the attitudes of early Christians toward it and toward the various media through which this authority presented itself to them. Any attempt at a more precise analysis would probably involve the risk of making a too subjective judgment. However, it is within the bounds of demonstrable fact to say that during the first three centuries of the Church the concept of authority, as mediated from God through the specific agencies which were regarded as representing his will and truth, tended steadily to move from a predominant (though not exclusive) emphasis upon what may be called "moral authority" and eyewitness authority toward emphasis upon the more legalistic and official type of authority.

We may be sure that the first Christians regarded the gospel, their faith in it, and the Church itself as resting firmly on the authority of God and Christ. This included the authority of history—the record of what God had done of old and what he had spoken through the prophets, and the convincing reports of what Jesus had done and said as this was delivered by those who had seen and heard him and a generation later by those who had received the message from the original witnesses. It included also all the dynamic events displaying the power of God, some of which they had seen and some of which they had learned about by credible testimony. The experience of their own changed lives and the observation of the changed lives of other Christians had firsthand evidential value. That the gospel was the "power of God" was not a proposition to be accepted at the command of an authorized officer; it was a fact that could be experienced and observed. One does not ask "by what authority" the sun causes vegetation to grow. Its power to produce that beneficent effect is its authority to do so. So these had seen and felt as well as heard about the power of God. "Power" is a more congenial concept than "authority" in the earliest Christian history. Paul uses the word *dunamis* (power) forty-six times in his epistles and *exousia* (authority) only twenty-seven times.

The whole picture [in Acts] . . . suggests a firm impression in the writer that the preaching of the Gospel and the emergence and development of the early Church were marked by striking manifestations of the active power of God, healing, guiding, judging, convicting and converting.[3]

But the infant Church and the new converts who were its members were not left to rely only upon casual reports of the great things that God had done and their own experience, observation, and interpretation of these things. The authority of God, of Christ, and of truth was mediated to them through channels which were objective to the individual as well as through his own experience. There were leaders and teachers, and there soon came to be norms and standards, which became proximate "authorities." The real problem about "authority" in the apostolic age and subsequently has to do with the channels or agencies through which the authority of God and of truth was believed to be mediated to the people, and with the development and transformation which these agencies underwent in the postapostolic period.

Customs and rites which are the integral parts of any group's oldest and most continuous tradition, and which are felt to be fraught with deep meaning, have a kind of assumed and unquestioned validity of their own. Members of the group have no feeling that these need the support of any other authority; they are themselves authorities. So it was with baptism and the Lord's Supper. For the Lord's Supper, Paul does, indeed, on one occasion (I Cor. 11:23 ff.) cite specific authority, but he does so not to justify its observance—which no one questioned —but to teach the proper mode and spirit in which it should be observed. There is not a hint anywhere in the New Testament that any Christian needed to have it proved to him that these two ceremonies were features of the Christian order.

[3] R. R. Williams, *Authority in the Apostolic Age* (London: SCM Press, 1950), pp. 86-87. Copyright 1950. Used by permission of The Macmillan Co. and S. C. M. Press.

They had been practiced ever since the Church had come into existence. The New Testament verses which furnished in later centuries the textual authority for these "sacraments" (as they came to be called) are rather records of the continuous and unquestioned practice of them than rules laid down for their observance. That they were taken for granted may explain why there is so little definition or explanation in the references to them.

As to baptism, there are indeed a good many references (seventeen in Paul's writings) from which all the facts that need to be known about it can be deduced. These may be summarized in the recent words of an Anglican scholar: "Baptism then, according to St. Paul, is a ceremony of immersion in water, and emergence from it, by means of which the convert is united to Christ in His death and resurrection, and enters that 'new creation' wherein those who are *en Christo* dwell." [4]

As to the Lord's Supper, the account of its institution as given in three Gospels is more detailed and explicit than any record of the institution of Christian baptism, but the references to it in Acts and the epistles are less frequent. They are, however, sufficient to show that the Church unquestionably regarded the Supper as a precious possession which it had always had. To quote again a summary by the same author, with special attention to the one extended reference (I Cor. 11):

At Corinth, in A.D. 55, there was established—though accompanied by considerable abuses—a sacramental meal, expressive of unity with Christ, in gratitude for, and appropriation of His sacrifice, leading to intimate union with those who equally partook of the meal and what it stood for. The validity of the Eucharist, it need hardly be said, was not thought to depend on questions of legal or ecclesiastical order, but on the right spirit in the members of the assembly (contrast Ignatius, Smyrn. viii. 1. "Let that be a valid Eucharist which is under the Bishop"). [5]

[4] *Ibid.*, p. 91.
[5] *Ibid.*, pp. 94-95.

Looking at the first three centuries of Christianity as a whole, we can say that the three media which were regarded, or which came to be regarded, as conveying to men the authority of God were these: first, certain chosen men, apostles, evangelists, prophets, persons with "spiritual gifts," and office-bearers in the church; second, certain Christian writings which ultimately became the New Testament; third, formulations of doctrine which were developed into the great creeds and confessions. Above all these gradually rose the authority of the Church itself. To that development we shall presently return. But first, what channels of authority were recognized in the apostolic age?

The authority exercised by the apostles over the Church was evidently not that of men who held offices which entitled them to obedience, but that of men whose exceptional opportunities for knowing the facts about the life and teachings of Jesus and about the gospel of salvation gave them the right to instruct others. Further, they were men of proved devotion to his cause and men who by their own account had been commissioned by him to spread this gospel. Moreover, they had "power" (*dunamis,* not *exousia*) , for it was reported and believed by all that they, together with the rest of the 120 on Pentecost, had received a special manifestation of the Holy Spirit and that some of them performed miracles. The one text (Matt. 16:19) which can be cited in support of authority to rule is of doubtful interpretation. Whatever it means, it applies only to Peter, who is directly addressed with a pronoun and verb in the singular number. It does not either explicitly or implicitly extend to the other eleven or to any possible "successors" of Peter or the others. But where the "binding and loosing" formula is repeated in Matt. 18:18, it is in the plural. Not only is there no evidence that Peter ever exercised any ruling authority; there is direct evidence that he did not. Acts 11:2 shows that Peter's decisions and acts could be challenged. The dissension at Antioch about circumcision was referred to Jerusalem—not to Peter but to the "apostles and elders" (Acts 15:2) . Peter stated the case to the whole Church, Paul and

Barnabas testified, James proposed the solution that was accepted, and the "apostles and elders and brethren" (15:23) gave the reply. The apostles themselves were no supreme court, no bench of bishops. When Peter later took a different position, Paul "withstood him to the face" (Gal. 2:11).

Only for a very short time did the apostles form a compact group, and the degree of their actual activity and co-operation, even in the earliest days, is conjectural. Most of them immediately dropped out of history. A week or two after the Resurrection, Matthias was chosen by lot to fill the vacancy caused by the defection of Judas, but the idea that the number of twelve must be kept full was dropped immediately. When James the son of Zebedee became an early martyr, no successor was appointed. Apparently only defection produced a vacancy; death did not, because the function of the Twelve was a celestial one, that of "judging the twelve tribes of Israel." When Matthias was chosen to take the place of Judas, it appeared that the only successor an apostle could have would be some other disciple who had "companied with us all the time that the Lord Jesus went in and out among us" (Acts 1:21). Peter was most conspicuous at first. James seems to have had a brief primacy of honor on the ground of his relationship with Jesus, but he was not an apostle. Matthew's fame is perpetuated by the Gospel to which his name is attached, but he is not mentioned in the book of Acts. John in Asia Minor and Paul were, so far as the New Testament or other authentic records go, the only other apostles who figured in the leadership of the Church. The phrase "the college of the apostles" represents nothing real or enduring. The fantastic legends of apostolic exploits, especially in the East and South, only show how much the Church later desired to magnify the apostolic office when the bishops had become "successors of the apostles"—and how little data it had to go on.

Yet the authority of the apostles (or of the few that we know anything about) as teachers and as founders of local churches was potent. Documentation of this statement depends almost wholly on the records of Paul's work, as given in Acts and in his epistles. It was only by an extension of the title "apostle" beyond the limit that Peter had defined (Acts 1:21) that Paul could claim it. It went even further than that, for Barnabas is called an apostle (Acts 14:14), and Andronicus and Junia were said to be "of note among the apostles" (Rom. 16:7), and the references to "false apostles" (II Cor. 11:13) and to those who "say they are apostles, and are not" (Rev. 2:2) clearly suggest that in the second and third generations of the Church the term "apostle" did not necessarily mean a member of a known and narrow group of twelve men but might be equivalent to "missionary." Paul's function and prestige were unique, so far as the historical evidence goes. He not only made converts and planted churches but watched over them as constantly as his travels permitted, wrote letters to them for their instruction and correction, and sometimes sent younger associates (like Timothy and Titus) to give them oversight.

There is but little factual data to show whether the churches themselves exercised any authority either by action of the whole body or by regularly appointed officers. The evidence does not indicate any uniform pattern of local organization. The early references to bishops, elders, and deacons are very few. Though some advocates of episcopacy hold that the "three-fold ministry" was a feature of the apostolic church, many others who are equally committed to episcopacy as an indispensable polity agree with the great majority of nonepiscopal scholars in saying that nothing of the kind can be found in the New Testament, that "bishop" and "elder" were two names for the same office, and that each city church normally had several of them. For example:

Bishops are indistinguishable from presbyters in the New Testament period. How the transition was made from the collegiate episcopacy [that is, presbyterate, or eldership] of Philippians (and 1 Clement) to the monepiscopacy of Ignatius we do not know. Later generations quite naturally turned to bishops for some of the functions which apostles had performed . . . , but we have no decisive information as to whether the original apostles had any hand in this development.[6]

But if there are difficulties in the way of proving that either Christ or his apostles instituted a "threefold ministry," it is almost equally hard to prove it for a twofold ministry. The "seven" at Jerusalem (Acts 6:1-6) had neither title nor official status, but only duties in connection with a peculiar local situation. They are nowhere called deacons. In fact, biblical mentions of deacons are extremely rare. Paul sends greetings to the "bishops and deacons" at Philippi (Phil. 1:1) and tells Timothy what qualifications deacons should have (I Tim. 3:8-13). That is all, and one of these is in a letter of disputed and probably later authorship.

Elders are mentioned much more often, but apparently not always as officers. The writer of the book of Acts moves without a break from references to the Jewish "elders and scribes," "chief priests and elders," and the "people and the elders and the scribes" to a mention of the "apostles and elders" at Jerusalem. When this phrase is repeated (Acts 15:23), the phrase in the Greek becomes "apostles and elder brothers." There is no account of the appointment of elders at Jerusalem. Acts 14:23 says that Paul "ordained . . . elders in every church" in Galatia, but he does not mention them in the letter which he wrote to those churches.

We know the church at Corinth better than any other apostolic church, but we find no reference anywhere to officers of any kind in it, though one would suppose Paul would have given some injunctions to the officers, if there had been any, in connection with his sharp criticism of the disorderly state of the church. On the contrary, he speaks of those who have "gifts," of the leadership that should be exercised by the early converts ("first fruits," or charter members), and of the representative whom he may send.

[6] *Ibid.*, p. 109.

The form and degree of organization of the churches in the apostolic age need not be further discussed in this connection. The subject has been exhaustively studied by many scholars, and all minds are not yet in entire agreement on the conclusions. My view, which I believe to come close to representing the consensus of scholarship, is that the polity of local churches was neither uniform nor authoritatively prescribed during that part of the apostolic age upon which the New Testament throws light; that "officers" as such had no large place in it; that there were various kinds of ministries (Paul mentions eight kinds in I Cor. 12:28) which, like the various members of the body, performed different specialized functions; that no church had any single administrative officer (bishop or other) who was regarded as the guardian of its faith, the custodian of the apostolic tradition, director of its activities, or even the permanent chairman of its council of presbyters; and that the dividing line between "clergy" and "laity" was so indistinct (I will not say nonexistent) that those terms cannot be used without importing into them the flavor which they derive from the later period when, as a matter of fact, they were actually coined.

If any reader disagrees with one or more of these findings, the main argument of this chapter is not thereby vitiated. The essential points, to which these characteristics of local church polity are merely accessory and illustrative, are these:

First, the local churches of the apostolic age had no uniform pattern of organization or clerical ministry which we are justified in regarding as mandatory. Those who regard the structure and practices of the churches founded by apostles as normative for all time—and therefore as essential features of a united Church in our time—cannot find here the authority for insistence upon any single pattern of organization or ministry. The precedent rather favors liberty and variety.

(The First Epistle of Clement of Rome, Chapters 42, 44, will be cited by those who think this leaves the organization too vague. The two possible interpretations of the text lend themselves, respectively, to the support of the episcopal and the presbyterial orders, but in any case it does not alter the picture of the apostolic age itself.)

Second, the Church as a whole had no unified or centralized organization. The apostles as a body did not constitute such a controlling authority, for outside Jerusalem they never acted as a body and there only briefly. The apostles individually did not exercise that kind of authority over the whole Church, though the travels and labors of some of them contributed much toward weaving the widely separated companies of Christians into a fellowship that included them all. The same sort of service was rendered by the men who traveled with Paul from time to time, such as Barnabas and Luke, and by his younger assistants, such as Timothy and Titus, and probably by other traveling evangelists. But the Church had no general officers, no district or diocesan authorities, no ecclesiastical apparatus of any kind for giving oversight to the local congregations, standardizing their faith and practice, or binding them into a united organization. Even if it could be shown that New Testament "bishops" were not identical with "presbyters" but were a distinct and higher grade of officers—thus providing the "threefold ministry" of bishops, presbyters, and deacons—still it would remain to be proved that the bishops had any jurisdiction outside their respective cities or any association or interchange of communication among themselves which could make them instruments of an organized unity of the whole Church. But for this, there is no evidence whatever.

The conclusion is inevitable that the human channels of authority—that is to say, the apostles and the ministry—were not instruments of organizational unity for the church of the apostolic age.

The other two possible channels of authority—the New Testament and the creeds—can be briefly dismissed so far as concerns the apostolic age. Neither of them existed at this period.

So far as the creeds are concerned, the statement can be left at that. They did not exist. Furthermore, the theological materials from which the great creeds were to be formulated did not yet exist in the mind of anyone. To be sure, Schaff says that

in a certain sense [italics mine] . . . the Christian Church has never been without a creed. . . . The baptismal formula and the words of institution of the Lord's Supper are creeds; these and the confession of Peter antedate even the birth of the Christian Church on the day of Pentecost. . . . If a man can say from his heart, "I believe in the Lord Jesus Christ," it is sufficient for his salvation.[7]

Such a confession was in substance the "creed" of the apostolic church. But it is only "in a certain sense" that this simple yet adequate confession can be called a creed. If the word is taken in the dictionary sense, which is also the sense in which Schaff uses it in his great work and the sense in which it is generally understood, as an "authoritative doctrinal formula," then the apostolic church did not yet have a creed. We have already considered the common faith in Jesus Christ as Lord, which was the fundamental unifying force in the church of the first century. The development of creeds elaborating that faith and adding specifications and particulars was the work of later generations.

Paul's letters contain much solid theological material, but this was in no sense a "creed" of the Church in his time. Goodspeed says they were "first published" (that is, made generally available to the churches) "not long before A.D. 95." [8] In the earliest postbiblical writings the emphasis was heavily on conduct rather than doctrine. Indeed, the way of love and fellowship *was* the doctrine. When the Didache says, "You shall keep the teachings you have received, neither adding to them nor taking from them," it sets this injunction in the midst of ex-

[7] Philip Schaff, *The Creeds of Christendom* (New York: Harper & Bros., 1877), I, 5.
[8] *Op. cit.*, pp. 2-3.

hortations to purity, generosity, piety, fasting, and prayer. Similarly, in the *Epistle of Barnabas*—the text of which is included in the Codex Sinaiticus, the oldest complete manuscript of the New Testament—there is much about meekness, liberality, purity, and love, little or nothing about what we would call doctrine. Orthodoxy in the theological sense came a little later as a defense against "heresy."

As to the New Testament, what I mean to say, of course, is that, though the writings (or most of them) existed, they did not yet constitute the New Testament. The unifying effect of the apostolic writings was second only to that of the faith itself. They communicated the faith, and they paralleled and extended the personal ministry of their writers. The churches which received letters from Paul must have felt the impact of his authority scarcely less than when he stood before them and spoke. But there is no reason to suppose that either the Jewish or the Gentile Christians at Rome, for example, when Paul's epistle arrived, realized that they were receiving a document destined to be included in a second volume of sacred scripture co-ordinate with the Old Testament, which they all reverenced. Nor is it likely that Paul himself took this view of the matter, fully convinced as he was that he was a chosen instrument in the hand of God and a messenger for Christ. Such thoughts imply no belittling of the importance or authority of the writings. For the continuing life of the Church, for the anchorage of its faith to the source and ground of that faith, and for our own knowledge of what the Church and its faith were in the apostolic age, nothing else could be as important as the New Testament. But when we are inquiring what were the factors which gave to the apostolic church such unity as it had, we cannot say that the New Testament was one of them. It is our source of information about the degree and kind of unity that existed, but it was not one of the causes of the condition which it describes. Loyalty to the New Testament cannot have been a characteristic of the New Testament church or a bond of unity for it.

This said, it must again be emphasized that there were literary channels of authority which together formed an indispensable ground for the Church's faith and a powerful force in binding it into one fellowship. These were: (1) the collections of sayings of Jesus and of partly standardized accounts of his deeds, which, first orally transmitted then doubtless written, furnished the literary materials from which the Gospels were to be compiled; and (2) the total mass of Christian writings that was building up through the first century, including those which were later received as genuinely apostolic and were collected to form the New Testament, and those which were put into a lower category of value or were discarded entirely.

The oral gospel tradition of the sayings and acts of Jesus was certainly the earliest of these. We do not know how early this began to be put into writing or how generally such collections circulated in their earliest written form. How many Christians besides the compilers of Matthew and Luke had access to Q? There is no evidence to support the claim, made later, that a continuous oral tradition, transmitted from bishops to their successors in churches that had been planted by apostles, gave to these bishops some special knowledge or insight superior to what the rest of the Church possessed. The unitive value of the oral tradition, so long as it remained oral, lay in the fact that so many scattered Christians and widely separated churches knew a good deal of it. When it was written, and especially when the written sources had been edited into the form of the Gospels as we have them, the oral tradition had done its work. There is no evidence that there was any of it left over to be the special possession of the bishops.

The one purpose of this condensed account of the Church in the apostolic age has been to exhibit, so far as they can be known, the essential facts about the degree and kind of unity it possessed and the things that gave it that unity.

In summary, we can say that the Church of the apostolic age was one Church. Devotion to one Lord and the sharing of a common hope gave a sense of fellowship among its widely scattered members. Some of them at least had received the teaching that in spite of distance in space and differences in race and culture they constituted what might be called in various figures of speech the body of Christ, or a body of which Christ was the head, or the bride of Christ, or a building of which Christ was the cornerstone. The issues upon which the Church was later to become divided had not yet arisen. But the many Christian communities were not yet united in any organizational way, or upon any theological statements of the implications of their faith, or under any administrative structure. In short, the visible Church was not divided but not yet united.

Chapter III

From Persecution to Freedom
UNITY BY EXCLUSION

THE DOUBLE TITLE OF THIS CHAPTER DERIVES FROM TWO IM-
portant features of the period with which it deals. The first is
that the Church was passing through the times of persecution
and into an era of freedom and even of imperial favor. The
second is that during the second and third centuries the Church
developed strongly the concept of "catholicity"—as implying
both universality and doctrinal orthodoxy—and began to practice the policy of maintaining both unity and uniformity by
expelling from its ranks as "heretics" or "schismatics" all who
deviated from the theological beliefs of the main body or
rejected the authority of its bishops. Since these were not
regarded as Christians at all and their congregations were
held to be not real churches, *the* Church was not divided when
they were cut off. This is what I am calling "unity by exclusion." This was perfectly feasible even when the Church had
no political influence or legal status and was still liable to
recurrent persecutions. It became more effective when during
the greater part of the fourth century the imperial power had
motives of its own for enforcing the unity of the Church even
before it took the final step of violently suppressing both
heretics and pagans.

The process of exclusion of course worked both ways. While
the churches that called themselves catholic were excluding
those regarded as heretical or schismatic, some of these latter

65

groups were just as actively separating themselves from the so-called orthodox.

Tertullian in his *De Praescriptione Haereticorum* (about A.D. 200) makes even more explicit the criteria of sound doctrine and good order which Irenaeus had stated a little earlier. A doctrine is catholic and authoritative if it is apostolic. It is apostolic if it is found in the writings of the apostles or in the "apostolic tradition" handed down in churches that have existed continuously from the days of the apostles. The bishops, being themselves in unbroken succession from the apostles, are the channels through which this tradition is transmitted and its only authorized custodians and interpreters. The injunction to "search the Scriptures" was viewed with some suspicion because independent searchers might arrive at unacceptable conclusions. Only what the bishops found in the apostolic writings and in the apostolic tradition constituted the *regula fidei*. Those who did not conform to this and those who did not acknowledge the authority of the "catholic" bishops who guaranteed it were outside the Church. So the Church remained united in spite of apparent divisions, because it consisted only of those who *were* united. This is unity by definition, or "unity by exclusion." The Church can always be in theological agreement if it is defined as consisting only of those who agree. The first clear statement of this policy, I believe, is that given in this work by Tertullian *On the Proscription of Heretics,* which the great Anglican scholar F. J. A. Hort called a "most plausible and mischievous book."

During the two and a half centuries following the close of the apostolic age—say from A.D. 100 to 350—some radical changes occurred in the condition, structure, doctrines, and status of the Church. Some of these changes affected the concept and character of its unity and its methods of attaining or preserving unity. Here also it will be useful to remember the three factors—fellowship, faith, and leadership, or authority—which furnished the outline under which we observed the unity of the Church in the first century. But now these three cannot

66

be so distinctly separated. A new type of leadership had appeared. The category of authority, as mediated through specific channels of ecclesiastical office, tended to dominate the scene. The Church's fellowship and its faith had lost none of their importance, but the shift was toward a condition in which both the character and the limits of Christian fellowship were determined by authoritative leaders of the Church, who were in effect its rulers, and in which the faith had become a body of doctrinal affirmations more sharply defined than any that had ever been stated by Jesus or his apostles.

It is unnecessary for the purpose of this book to attempt to describe the steps by which these changes took place. The historical evidence is not sufficient to give a clear picture of all the successive stages in the process, and there are some not unreasonable differences of opinion. Some scholars have called the latter part of the first century and the first half of the second century a "dark tunnel" in the Church's history—not dark, of course, to the people who were living through it, but obscure to our observation because of our lack of adequate documentary data about it. The Church entered that "tunnel" with the characteristics indicated in the preceding pages. It came out as the "catholic Church"—not Roman Catholic but "catholic" in a new sense and with criteria of catholicity, and therefore of fellowship, which were previously unknown.

As an illustration of the obscurity which befogs this period, we may take one topic that is one of the sensitive spots in all present union efforts. An Anglican writer says: "Bishops are indistinguishable from presbyters in the New Testament period. How the transition was made from the collegiate episcopacy [that it, the plural eldership, or presbyterate] of Philippians (and I Clement) to the monepiscopacy of Ignatius we do not know." [1] Just as little do we know how the next step occurred, the extension of the bishop's jurisdiction from a single congregation to a diocese. But these are things that we certainly ought

[1] Williams, *op. cit.*, p. 109.

to know if the resulting arrangement is to be regarded as permanently indispensable to either the *esse* or the *bene esse* of the Church. Many defenders of episcopacy as *de facto* the best system of polity share the confession of ignorance quoted above. Many, however, do not share it but on the contrary hold that the system was in existence from the beginning in the purpose of God and in the commission given by Christ. Whichever one of these views may be right, the fact that such a difference exists even among those who support the episcopal system (not to mention those who reject it) indicates the tenuous and inconclusive character of the historical evidence that might either prove that the system was at least authorized by the apostles or disclose and justify the steps by which it was developed.[2]

We may as well face at once the most crucial and controversial question in regard to these changes in the structure and functioning of the Church. Everyone admits that there were changes. The question is: What do these changes mean, and what authority, if any, do they have for the Church of later times, including our own? Three quite different answers are possible: (1) that the men who guided the destinies of the Church willfully and sinfully departed from a divinely authorized pattern, so that the changes they made should be repudiated and reversed and the *status quo ante* restored; (2) that the Church and its leaders, exercising the liberty they had in the absence of any authorized pattern, developed modes of expression and procedure which may have served a good purpose in their time but are open to legitimate change to meet the needs of a later time; or (3) that the Holy Spirit so dwelt in the Church and

[2] Hugh Martin in *Christian Reunion* quotes William Temple, then archbishop of York, later of Canterbury, as saying in a published lecture that the form or forms of the ministry in the first two centuries cannot be certainly known but that it is "at least highly probable" that the ministry was normally passed along by a system of continuous succession, and that it is certain that the episcopal ministry was the only one in the field by the end of the second century. This seems a careful and conservative statement of the historical basis of the "divine right of episcopacy" by one who thoroughly believed in that system.

guided its decisions that the changes (or "developments") of that period in doctrine and polity were the work not of men but of God and are therefore permanently binding as being of the *esse* of the Church.

The first of these three answers states the presupposition underlying most of the attempts to "restore primitive Christianity." This with some important differences of interpretation and application has been the common characteristic of most reformatory movements. Partisans of the other two views often describe it critically, if not contemptuously, as a futile attempt at the "repristination" of the Church. The problem this view presents is twofold: (1) to determine with certainty exactly what the primitive Church did, for example, in the matter of baptism or the structure of the ministry; and (2) to decide how much of what the primitive Church did was intended to be part of that permanent pattern which the Church of all ages should follow. Scholarly opinions differ in both of these areas, and from these differences many divisions in the Church have resulted, even among those who share this answer to the main question.

The second answer has the defect or merit—according to the point of view from which it is evaluated—of presenting the actual and objective Church as a social institution immersed in the stream of cultural evolution and constituting a part of that stream. The defenders of this view need not, and generally do not, say that this is a complete description of the Church, for it has a gospel and a fellowship which are not mere sociological facts. It is the intellectual formulation of the faith and the forms of the Church's structure and worship that they hold to be within the area of Christian liberty and therefore subject to reconsideration and revision from time to time, and also to possible diversity at any given time. However, they suffer the forensic disadvantage of not being able to support any extended declaration of faith or program of polity by affixing to it the seal of divine approval and declaring that it is ultimate and absolute. They do enjoy the advantage of being on easy terms of fellowship with any Christians who are willing to be in fellowship with them.

The third answer makes much of what its spokesmen call the "witness of history," sometimes forgetting that history only bears witness to what has happened and that other than historical criteria must be applied to determine whether it ought to have happened and whether it was man or God who made it happen. The hypothesis that the doctrinal and structural changes in the Church during its first three centuries were necessarily Spirit-directed raises a further question in the inquiring mind. If the changes made in the second, third, and fourth centuries are to be ascribed to the agency of the Holy Spirit, why not those made or to be made in the twentieth century? How ascribe finality to the Spirit's work of revision in, say, the fourth century if the same Spirit is still at work? Is not the quest in history for a permanent norm of creed and polity defeated by the very method adopted for guaranteeing it by the "witness of history"?

To return to the changes themselves: Though the fellowship among Christians was colored and controlled by the authorities which had risen to power in the Church, the reality and the fundamentally spiritual nature of that fellowship must not be underestimated. The new bonds among Christians did not take the place of the old sense of brotherhood among the followers of Christ but were added to it. As a fellowship of believers the Church certainly has an unbroken and undisputed continuity. The documentation of that fact, even through the "dark tunnel" and through the years of organizational consolidation after it, is adequate and convincing.

The "old Jerusalem gospel" of mutual aid, reflected in Acts 4:32, was reaffirmed in Doctrina (the earliest form of the Didache) about A.D. 100: "You shall not turn away the needy, but shall share everything with your brethren." Scarcely one of the postapostolic writers fails to reinforce this injunction, even when, as in the Didache itself, it is deemed necessary to give warning against imposters. Even here, the warning is against persons who claimed special consideration on the false pretense that they were "prophets" rather than against any danger of being too generous toward needy brothers. Even some of the enemies of Christianity and the relatively neutral observers noted favorably, though they could not understand, this sense of family solidarity among the Christians. Significant is the reluctant testimony of the "apostate" Emperor Julian (331-63) who, in promoting a pagan revival, tried to shame the pagans into more humane ways by saying that nobody but the Christians had any care for the needy and sick or showed any hospitality to travelers. By that date Christianity had become the officially favored religion of the empire and had, by persuasion or otherwise, gained a vast number of adherents. The old sense of intimate brotherhood inevitably suffered such change as must occur when a small group becomes a large one and when many persons are brought into it by motives extraneous to its central purpose. But still there were evident signs of that brotherly love which from the first had been the corollary of their faith and of their devotion to their Master.

No matter what theory one holds in regard to the antiquity of the episcopate and its relation to the apostolic office, it is beyond question that the importance of bishops increased greatly during the second century and that there was no recorded protest against this development. Defenders of episcopacy are entitled to have full weight given to this latter fact. The classic passages in regard to the episcopate are in the Didache, I Clement, and the epistles of Ignatius, all written not long after A.D. 100.

Elect, therefore, for yourselves bishops and deacons worthy of the Lord, humble men and not covetous, and faithful and well tested; for they also serve you in the ministry of the prophets and teachers. Do not, therefore, despise them, for they are the honored men among you, along with the prophets and teachers. (Didache, 15.) [3]

[3] Didache, tr. Francis X. Slimm, in *The Apostolic Fathers* (New York: Christian Heritage, Inc., 1947), p. 183.

This clearly reflects conditions at a time when the chief dependence of the Church was upon men who were regarded as
Spirit-chosen, possessors of "spiritual gifts," and when it could
be feared that leaders who were humanly chosen for a ministry
in the Church would not be properly respected.

The Apostles received the Gospel for us from the Lord Jesus
Christ; Jesus Christ was sent from God. Christ, therefore, is from
God and the Apostles are from Christ. Both, accordingly, came
in proper order by the will of God. . . . Preaching, accordingly,
throughout the country and the cities, they appointed their first-
fruits, after testing them by the Spirit, to be bishops and deacons of
those who should believe. . . . Our Apostles also knew, through
our Lord Jesus Christ, that there would be contention over the
bishop's office. So, for this cause, having received complete fore-
knowledge, they appointed the above-mentioned men, and afterwards gave them a permanent character, so that, as they died,
other approved men should succeed to their ministry. Those,
therefore, who were appointed by the Apostles or afterwards by
other eminent men, with the consent of the whole Church, and
who ministered blamelessly to the flock of Christ in humility,
peaceably and nobly, being commended for many years by all—
these men we consider are not justly deposed from their ministry.
(I Clement, 42:1-2, 4; 44:1-3.) [4]

Even more emphatic in regard to the bishop as the guardian
of the truth and the center of the church's unity is Ignatius,
who is always called bishop of Antioch, though he never speaks
of himself as a bishop. These are some of his strongest expressions:

It is right for you to concur, as you do, with the mind of the
bishop. For your [presbyters], who are worthy of the name and
worthy of God, like the strings of a lyre, are in harmony with the
bishops. (To the Ephesians 4.)
It ill becomes you to treat your bishop too familiarly because

[4] *I Clement*, in *ibid.*, pp. 42-44.

of his youth. You should show him all reverence out of respect for the authority of God the Father. (To the Magnesians 3.)

Just as the Lord, being one with the Father, did nothing, either in His own person or through the Apostles, without the Father, so you should do nothing without the bishop and the council of [presbyters]. (To the Magnesians 7.)

For it seems to me that, when you are obedient to the bishop as you would be to Jesus Christ, you are living, not in a human way, but according to Jesus Christ, who died for us that by faith in His death you might escape death. You must continue, then, to do nothing apart from the bishop. . . . In the same way all should respect the deacons as they would Jesus Christ, just as they respect the bishop as representing the Father and the [presbyters] as the council of God and the college of the Apostles. Apart from these there is nothing that can be called a Church. (To the Trallians 2, 3.) [5]

It is impossible not to observe how violently these passages, especially those from Ignatius, contrast with the scanty reference to bishops, presbyters, and deacons in the New Testament; but it is equally impossible in the light of these quotations not to realize how early these clerical orders began to acquire the prestige which presently made them—and uniquely the episcopate—the structural members of the edifice of the Church, the cement which maintained its unity, the judges of its growing system of doctrine, the administrators of its discipline, and ultimately, as the concept of priesthood became attached to them, the intermediaries between man and God.

It appears that the first function of the bishops as such was administrative rather than priestly. It had to do with disciplining offenders, deciding whether persons who "lapsed" under persecution were entitled to reinstatement when they professed penitence, and handling funds contributed for the relief of the poor, the sick, the aged, the orphans, travelers and visitors, and the often mentioned "virgins and widows." Institutions were established a little later for each of these classes,

[5] Tr. Gerald G. Walsh, in *ibid.*, pp. 88-89, 96, 98, 102-3.

and this vast system of relief and social security was doubtless one reason why Christianity won so many converts. The bishops carried the chief responsibility for all this. Moreover, their office gained prestige as they became "guardians of the unity of the Church" (to quote Ramsey) by being the representatives of their communities in correspondence with other Christian communities and in the informal conferences among neighboring churches out of which the first councils developed. The Roman provinces furnished the geographical pattern for such councils. They did not become important until the time of Cyprian (who died A.D. 258), and even he insisted that these councils had no authority, even over their own minorities. But if they did not speak with authority, certainly their decisions carried weight, for they were the consensus of groups of bishops all of whom were deemed to be legitimate channels of the apostolic tradition and by their consecration to be endowed with a special grace which equipped them to transmit it without corruption.

By the middle of the third century, then, the Church's original consciousness of its heavenly or ideal unity as the body of Christ and the fellowship of believers had been supplemented by a sense of need for an earthly and organizational unity. The development of the episcopate was the most important factor in meeting this need. This involved certain concrete and visible facts, paralleling the growth of a theory of the origin and special sacredness of the episcopal office. These historical facts were: (1) the elevation of one presbyter-bishop above the others and his designation as *the* bishop of the local church; (2) the extension of the bishop's jurisdiction to cover the area surrounding the town in which his home church was located; (3) the establishment of understandings and agreements among the bishops of a district through correspondence, visits, messengers, and meetings; (4) a gradation of bishops in dignity and prestige based on the recognition of superior status for bishops of important cities and for those whose home churches had been founded by apostles.

The claim of the bishop of Rome to an absolute primacy over all other bishops and absolute sovereignty over the whole Church was later to become the ground of a still more solid institutional unity for the western Church. But by the time that claim had gained general acceptance in the West, the East was already drawing away. The plane of cleavage was developing which was later to split the Church into two major segments. Even in the West the sovereignty of the Roman bishop was not unchallenged. Cyprian as bishop of Carthage promoted councils of the bishops of north Africa to voice their united protest against the arrogant claims of Rome. So the institutional unity of the Church was advanced locally even by organization for resistance to what was to become the medieval system of unity.

Other questions about which district or provincial councils of bishops consulted were such as these: the treatment of the "lapsed," those who had burned incense to the emperor or denied Christ under stress of persecution, and traditores who had surrendered copies of the Scriptures; the question of recognizing the validity of baptism by heretics; the even more fundamental decision as to who were heretics.

For heresies had arisen: that is, diverse views about God and Christ and the nature of the cosmos and man and the process of salvation.[6] The word "heresy" means personal opinion or free choice. To call anything a heresy is to imply that there is a collective or authoritative judgment on the matter under consideration, a standard of doctrine approved by authorities regarded as competent to make a statement for which no individual might presume to substitute his own opinion.

The existence of such a standard in regard to some matters, and of deviations from it, is clearly indicated in the apostolic age. But what was the nature and scope of that standard? At Corinth the principal heresies seem to have been quarrelsome-

[6] The best recent treatment of these heresies is to be found in S. L. Greenslade, *Schism in the Early Church* (London: Student Christian Movement Press, and New York: Harper and Bros., 1953).

ness and personal rivalries (I Cor. 11:18-21), and the standard by which these were to be corrected was a plain factual account of the origin of the Lord's Supper and an exhortation to self-examination and mutual consideration. The heresies against which the Galatians are warned (5:19-22) are moral rather than theological errors, classed as "works of the flesh" along with murder, adultery, and drunkenness, and all these are contrasted with the "fruits of the Spirit" such as "love, joy, peace, longsuffering, gentleness, goodness, faith, meekness, temperance." Tit. 3:10 (which may have been written by Paul ten years later or may have been written by someone else at the end of the century) gives the first injunction for really drastic treatment: "A man that is an heretick after the first and second admonition reject"; but here the heretic seems to be the man who persistently and contentiously raises the wrong questions rather than the one who gives the wrong answers. With II John 7 (about A.D. 100) and II Pet. 2:1 (perhaps as late as A.D. 150) we come into the age of real heresies in the sense now given to that word—denials of Christ's bodily reality or of his redemptive act. If these destructive doctrinal vagaries did not arise within what can be strictly called the apostolic age, they were certainly in conflict with the authorities which had been recognized in that period, namely, the personal testimony of the apostles themselves, their undisputed writings, and the Church's unanimously held tradition of faith, worship, and sacraments.

The second and third centuries saw the rise of other diversities of opinion on less crucial points of doctrine, and of more rigorous standards of orthodoxy supported by new types of authority and enforced by new sanctions.

One new authority was the New Testament. Its contents (with the probable exception of II Peter) had all been written by about the end of the first century, but many other writings competed for acceptance by the churches. M. R. James in *The Apocryphal New Testament* lists more than twenty "Gospels," about a dozen books of "Acts" of various apostles, six epistles, and five "Apocalypses"; and these do not include the many others which were from the first manifestly spurious or heretical. In addition some of the most honored books of the apostolic fathers (Clement, Barnabas, and Hermas) are found in the oldest New Testament manuscripts. Eusebius in the fourth century was still listing the Didache as possibly canonical though disputed. But the situation was not as confused as this would make it appear. Paul's letters had been collected before A.D. 100 and were everywhere accepted. By the end of the second century the four Gospels that we know were universally received, and Irenaeus had argued that in the eternal nature of things there could be neither more nor less than four (though one other still had strong supporters). The book of Acts was unquestioned. Disputes about the canon thereafter dealt with marginal issues—a few doubtful books and a few possible additions—rather than with the main body. There *was* a New Testament, and it was regarded as having primary authority or, more properly, as being a primary channel of the authority of God.

The other new authority, as has already been indicated, was the consensus of the more influential bishops. As an authority for the building of a more extensive body of doctrine which could become a creed and for consolidating the Church around a doctrinal position, the bishops had some advantages over the New Testament. They could claim authority for their interpretations of the New Testament and could reinforce this by reference to the unwritten apostolic tradition of which they were said to be the conservators. Actually I cannot find that much reliance was placed on this claim to the possession of an oral and unpublished tradition of teaching direct from the apostles. The occasional mentions of it seem to have been intended chiefly to undercut the claims of some of the heretics to be in possession of a body of secret apostolic teaching orally transmitted. It was as though the bishops were saying: If there is an oral tradition of the apostolic doctrine, who could be reasonably expected to have it—you free-lance philosophers

77

and migratory messengers from nowhere or we who are in the successions of chosen leaders of churches founded by the apostles? Yet there was in this period the beginning of a concept of "tradition" which was destined to have great importance —the idea that the definition and transmission of Christianity were not committed exclusively to a book, to which any literate person can refer and from which he can learn the whole truth about it, but that it was primarily entrusted to the Church, which was empowered both to preserve it uncorrupted and to interpret and develop it, so that the main stream of the Church's teaching *is* pure Christianity. The bishops were not only the principal agents in transmitting and enriching this tradition. They were in a position to deal with new questions as they arose. They could rally the churches to take action for the protection of the purity of the faith by the expulsion of "heretics," and later by invoking the aid of the civil power to make this expulsion more effective.

We have passed over with little attention one of the earliest and most serious threats to the unity of the Church—the tension, and to some extent the alienation, between Jewish and Gentile Christians. The old theory that Peter and Paul headed two bitterly warring parties has been so thoroughly exploded that it need not be discussed. The earliest Christian leaders had to make a great decision as to whether Christianity was Judaism plus something or was a new program to which Judaism had been preparatory in history but was not a prerequisite for the individual Christian. The book of Acts presents the issue clearly, credits Peter with taking the first liberalizing step and then becoming more cautious for fear of offending Jewish Christians, and pictures Paul as going the whole way in evangelizing the Gentiles while still maintaining his own status as a Jew as well as a Christian. Paul's letters show that his quarrel was not with the Jews but with the "Judaizers" who wanted the Gentiles to become Jewish proselytes before they could become Christian converts. There is no evidence that Peter or any other apostle ever took such a position. The problem, however, was a very real one as to how much of the Hebrew ideology and even of the Jewish religious program should pass over into the Christian faith, cultus, and polity, and how to maintain the unity of a Church in which there were different views and attitudes on these matters. Within the second century the extremists of both sides—the Ebionites as intransigent Judaizers and the Marcionites as radical rejectors of everything Jewish—were alike regarded as heretics outside the Church.

The more moderate Jewish and Gentile Christians seem to have worked out a compromise. This was the easier because the Jews of the Dispersion had become to a great extent Hellenized.[7] In the development of this compromise, for example, baptism came to be regarded as a substitute for circumcision, as apparently it never was in New Testament times. The Gentiles were satisfied that the ancient rite was discontinued; the moderate Judaizers were pleased that the continuity of the covenant was recognized by having something put "in the place" of circumcision, so that baptized (though uncircumcized) Gentiles might be considered as "proselytes of the gate." The practice of infant baptism introduced into Christianity the hereditary principle of Judaism. A little later, in the fourth century, the total-population theory of church membership was an adoption of the Hebrew concept of compulsory conformity by the whole community, in place of the Pauline (and also Petrine) reliance upon the faith of the individual as the criterion of his fitness for membership. The development of the orders of the clergy owed something to the Hebrew pattern, presbyters becoming "priests" and deacons corresponding to the Levites.

It was the concept of Christianity as a universal religion offered to men for their individual belief that won converts among the Gentiles and enabled the Church to gain a foot-

[7] See the surprising amount of evidence in the four volumes by Erwin R. Goodenough *Jewish Symbols in the Greco-Roman Period* (New York: Pantheon Books, Inc., 1953, 1954).

hold throughout the Graeco-Roman world. But it was a modification of the Judaizing tendency that took over and determined the character of the Church from the fourth century on. The later books in the New Testament canon, the apostolic fathers, and ante-Nicene fathers exhibit various aspects of the mediating process from one side or the other—for example, Hebrews, Clement of Rome, Tertullian, Cyprian. The resultant—an ecclesiastical edifice incorporating the main features of Judaism built on a foundation laid by the missionaries of a universal Christianity—was the "Catholic Church," which was about to become "Roman" by the final addition of a high priest who by one of history's strange anomalies was to take his title as "Pontifex Maximus" not from the line of Aaron or Zadok but from the Roman emperors in their capacity as supreme priest of the pagan religion.

Through all the changes which have been described—changes in the structure and polity of the church, in its methods of administration, in its criteria of orthodoxy, in its ways of dealing with persons who were heretics as judged by these new standards of doctrinal soundness, and consequent changes in the nature of its unity—through all these the Church remained an illegal religion, a small minority in an overwhelmingly pagan population, and liable to recurrent persecution by the Roman authorities. Serious as these persecutions were, they were quantitatively less than is generally supposed. The catacombs, which millions of vistors to Rome have seen, and the cult of the saints, which has glorified and canonized many of the martyrs of those early centuries, have given a somewhat exaggerated impression. It is probable that there was no appreciable amount of persecution in more than thirty of the nearly three hundred years before the Edict of Toleration, and the number of victims was a very small fraction of one per cent of the total number of Christians. The last two great persecutions—under Decius (250-51) and under Diocletian (303) —were the worst.

Yet the inferior legal status and the precarious security of

Christians, even when there was no immediate danger of death, evoked reasonable protest from Christian writers. Their pagan enemies had first charged them with specific crimes, but these charges never carried much weight even with the pagan populace. Omitting many details which are unnecessary for our purpose, we can say that the indictment against the Christians was that they refused to uphold the spiritual—or one might say, the mystical—unity of the Empire by paying divine honors to the emperor. The Romans were notoriously tolerant in matters of religion. They were hospitable to all the cults of the East. The Egyptian gods had many devotees. Half the army were worshipers of Mithra. One could have what new or strange gods one pleased. No one got into trouble either by worshiping these or by being frankly skeptical, as most educated Romans were, about the classic Olympian gods which had been borrowed from Greece and acclimated in Rome under other names—Jupiter for Zeus, Mars for Ares, and so on. The only important thing was that one should also make proper acknowledgment of the divine status of the emperor. The title "Divus Augustus" was not intended, as I understand it, to be an affirmation that the individual who held the office at the moment was of heavenly origin. Suetonius' popular *Lives of the Twelve Caesars* gives no hint of such an idea and is wholly inconsistent with it. Besides, the Romans knew too well the lowly derivation of some of them and how they had shot their way to the top through the Praetorian Guard. But the Romans had a philosophy of history according to which Rome itself—first the people, then the city, then the empire—was something like a perfect and eternal Platonic Idea, something like a heaven-born Child of Destiny, something like a pagan "City of God." Whoever became its ruler acquired ex officio this vaguely supernatural quality. To burn incense on the altar of *Divus Augustus* was therefore a way of giving an oath of allegiance to *Diva Roma,* and to refuse to do so was equivalent to refusing a loyalty oath. This was all that remained of the old idea, common to the Jews and many pagan peoples

81

and soon to be adopted by the Christian Church and the Christianized empire, that a state cannot survive unless all its citizens profess one religion. The persecuting emperors retained only a vestige of this idea, but they held that vestige tenaciously. The more precarious the state of the empire became, the more imperative the necessity of keeping at least this much of its religious unity. So thought Decius and Aurelian and Diocletian.

What did the Christians think of the effort of the pagan empire to preserve what remained of its own cultural unity and social integration by suppressing the religion which would not yield even such a minimum of acknowledgment to its spiritual claims? Naturally, they did not think well of it. They based their argument against persecution primarily on the grounds that they were in fact loyal subjects of the emperor, that Christianity was not a subversive movement, that the teaching and practice of Christian morality tended to check the forces which were corrupting the social order, and that the Christian doctrine had, as the apologists all along contended, the unique advantage of being true. All this was quite to be expected. More surprisingly there arose also voices asserting that the use of force either to compel or to prevent the exercise of any form of religion is inherently immoral, unreasonable, and ineffective. This latter line of defense against persecution by appeal to the individual man's natural right to choose his own religion—a line which the Church used when it was weak—should be remembered for comparison with the policy it adopted the moment it became both free and strong.

No one expressed these noble sentiments of religious toleration by the state more eloquently than that same Tertullian who had been so insistent on the excommunication of heretics by the Church. In his *Ad Scapulam* he wrote:

It is a fundamental human right, a privilege of nature, that every man should worship according to his own convictions: one man's religion neither harms nor helps another man. It is assuredly no part of religion to compel religion—to which free-will and not force should lead us. . . . You will render no real service to your gods by compelling us to sacrifice. For they can have no desire of offerings from the unwilling, unless they are animated by a spirit of contention, which is a thing altogether undivine. (Ch. ii.)

John Locke said much the same thing about fifteen hundred years later in his *Letters Concerning Toleration*. Again in his *Apology,* Tertullian wrote:

See that you do not give a further ground for the charge of irreligion by taking away religious liberty and forbidding free choice of deity, so that I may no longer worship according to my inclination, but am compelled to worship against it. Not even a human being would care to have unwilling homage rendered him.

Tertullian died, an old man, in A.D. 220, according to recent writers. He had seen many heretics, had written many books to confute them, and doubtless believed that they were headed for hell; but he would have abhorred the idea of compelling them to conform to the doctrines of the Church even if he had had the power to compel. Just as little would he have forced the pagans to cease worshiping their gods or to become Christians. Being himself a member of a religious minority, he was in a position to appreciate the beauty of toleration and the value of religious liberty.

Almost a century later, just before Constantine gave the Church its charter of freedom in the Edict of Milan (A.D. 313), the same idea was expressed even more forcibly by an apologist of immense popularity and prestige, Lucius Caelius Firmianus, more commonly known as Lactantius. In his *Institutiones Divinae* (Bk. V, chap. 20), speaking of the pagans and their violent measures against the Christians, especially in the Diocletian persecutions, which he had witnessed, he says:

Let their priests come forth. . . . Let them call us together to an assembly. . . . Let them show how the origins and beginnings of their sacred rites and gods were handed down to mortals. . . . There is no occasion for violence and injury, for religion cannot be imposed by force; the matter must be carried on by words rather than by blows, that the will may be affected. Let them unsheath the weapon of their intellect; if the system is true, let it be asserted. We are prepared to hear, if they teach; while they are silent, we certainly pay no credit to them, as we do not yield to them even in their rage. Let them imitate us in setting forth the system of the whole matter; for we do not entice, as they say; but we teach, we prove, we show. . . .

Torture and piety are widely different; nor is it possible for truth to be united with violence, or justice with cruelty. . . . But, they say, the public rites of religion must be defended. Oh, with what an honourable inclination the wretched men go astray! . . . Religion is to be defended, not by putting to death, but by dying; not by cruelty, but by patient endurance; not by guilt, but by good faith. . . . For if you wish to defend religion by bloodshed, and by tortures, and by guilt, it will no longer be defended, but will be polluted and profaned. For nothing is so much a matter of free-will as religion; in which, if the mind of the worshiper is disinclined to it, religion is at once taken away, and ceases to exist.

So this was what the Church wanted about the year A.D. 300, if the words of Lactantius can be taken as representing the general opinion, and there is not the slightest documentary evidence that it wanted anything else from the government. It wanted liberty for all men to make free choice of religion. It was willing to take its chances in the open forum of conscience and intelligence. It asked no favors for itself and no restraint for its competitors. "Nothing is so much a matter of free will as religion," and it felt that if truth and error were alike set free to fight it out, truth would prevail. The Church was still an absolutely voluntary society. Its appeal was in the truth it taught, the good lives of its members, and the works of mercy and benevolence that it did. Recurrent persecution still made it dangerous to be a Christian, but every man was perfectly free to join the Church or to stay out of it as his own choice might direct, just as in the days of Peter and Paul, and just as Tertullian and Lactanius said that every man ought to be free in the matter of religion.

Very soon the Church got just what it wanted. Constantine and his coemperor Licinius issued in A.D. 313 the Edict of Milan, which officially ended the persecution of Christianity. Professedly it ended all persecution in the field of religion. Here are some of the edict's generous phrases:

Liberty of worship shall not be denied to any, but the mind and will of every individual shall be free to manage divine affairs according to his choice. . . . Every person who desires to observe the Christian religion shall freely and unconditionally proceed to observe the same without let or hindrance. The same free and open power to follow their own religion or worship is granted also to others, in accordance with the tranquility of our times, in order that every person may have free opportunity to worship the object of his choice.

That might have been a clumsy draft for a section of the American Bill of Rights or the Statute of Virginia for Religious Freedom. What is more important in this connection is that it matches precisely the demand of Lactantius, written not more than ten years earlier, for complete freedom for every man to choose his own religion, whether Christian or pagan.

The parallel is so perfect that there is ground for a not unreasonable conjecture that Lactantius himself may have drafted the document for the emperor to sign. This is only a guess, and I do not remember seeing the suggestion elsewhere, but it has some plausibility—as a conjecture. In his pagan days Lactantius had been a popular professor of rhetoric. The Emperor Diocletian greatly admired him and brought him to his new capital, Nicomedia, to teach and lecture there. Soon after his conversion, which occurred between A.D. 300 and 313, Lactantius had written the book containing the strong appeal for general toleration which was quoted above. He was a friend of Constantine, who, as soon as he gained supreme power in the West, summoned him to Gaul to take charge of the education of his son, whom he designated to become his successor. It is not inherently improbable that this able rhetorician who had moved in imperial circles before his conversion, who had written eloquently in favor of religious liberty, and who had enjoyed the confidence of Constantine after his own and shortly before Constantine's conversion may actually have written the text of the edict which Constantine signed.

It was a great day in the history of Christianity when this charter of liberty closed the long and bloody record of the persecution of Christians by pagans. But it was not a major watershed in the history of the Church. It marked a notable change in the *fortunes* of the Church, but no change at all in its *character*. Before the edict of 313 it had been a Church composed of believers who had freely made their commitment to Christ and chosen the fellowship of the faithful. After the edict for a time it was the same kind of Church. The difference was that this choice could now be made without fear of penalties or persecution. It was still a free choice and a voluntary commitment. Gradually during the century which began with the Edict of Toleration and decisively near the end of that century, came the really revolutionary change which was a continental divide in the history of the Church and in the story of its unity. This was the change by which "orthodox" Christianity became a compulsory religion for the entire population of the empire. This change was revolutionary because it radically altered the character of the Church and the nature of its unity.

Because historians, and the Church itself, have generally been more interested in the Church's fortunes than in its character, Constantine's grant of toleration has been head-lined in the histories as the opening of a new epoch, while the Church's alliance with the state to utilize the police power for the suppression of all competing religions and unauthorized doctrines and by compulsion to make the membership of the Church coextensive with the total population—this radical revolution has been relegated to fine print. Yet this change in the character of the Church and in the nature of its relation to individuals and to society was the major determinant not only of the entire medieval system but also of the policies of classical Protestantism during the Reformation and for a long time after, and the consequences of it still linger to complicate and confuse the patterns of religion to this very day. A great part of the ecumenical effort of our own times is devoted to trying to overcome some of the disastrous effects of that revolution while refusing to recognize that it ever happened or that it was a revolution.

Since the theme of this book, in so far as it is historical, is the history of the Church's concept and quest of unity, let us summarize the developments during its first three centuries. The unity of the early Church began as a fellowship of the followers of Jesus, resting solely on faith in him as Lord and Savior. This faith was supported by the authority of Christ himself as mediated to believers by the testimony of apostles and other witnesses, by their own experience and observation of lives transformed by the power of God through the gospel, and by the practice and worship of churches which had received the gospel from its source. This fellowship of committed believers constituted the Church, which, they were taught, was the body of Christ. It had only rudimentary local organizations and no general organization whatever, but a sense of common cause was a very real bond among the scattered Christian communities and made them one Church whose common faith was that "Jesus is Lord."

At the beginning of the fourth century the unity of the Church still included a fellowship of believers sharply contrasted with the unbelieving world, but it was no longer merely a fellowship, and it was not a fellowship of all believers. A standardized body of doctrine had been developed, still far from complete but much more elaborated than the simple faith of the first Christians. The Church had now a well-developed system of organization and government, a structure of officials exercising authority over it and claiming to do so by the authority of Christ himself. Both doctrinal and disciplinary differences had arisen. Those Christians who accepted the doctrinal and disciplinary decisions of the principal bishops and their district councils called themselves the Catholic Church. Those who did not were excluded as heretics or schismatics. The Church was held to consist solely of those who were united in and under this doctrinal and ecclesiastical system. The Church was united because it consisted only of those who were willing to be united on that basis.

This chapter may end, as it began, with a reminder that, whatever changes the Church may have undergone in its first three centuries, it was still voluntary. The unity of the Church was the unity of those who by their own conviction and in the exercise of their own free will accepted membership in the Church as it was. That also was soon to be changed.

Chapter IV

The First Great Revolution
UNITY BY COMPULSION

CONSTANTINE'S EDICT OF MILAN IN A.D. 313 GAVE TOLERA-
tion to all religions. It thus changed both the policy and the
character of the Roman Empire, but it did not change the
character of the Church or the nature of its unity. Changes
in the Church began soon and reached their completion, at
least in theory, before the end of the century. The distinction
between these two historical events has been blurred if not entirely overlooked by most writers on the period, but it is clearly
stated by a recent archbishop of York:

> With the so-called Edict of Milan the persecutions came to an
> end. "For the first time in history, the principle of universal
> toleration was officially laid down—that every man has a right to
> choose his religion and to practise it in his own way without any
> discouragement from the State." [*Cambridge Mediaeval History*,
> Vol. I, p. 5.] . . . But it was not until sixty-two years later that
> Christianity became the established religion of the Empire, when
> Theodosius issued an edict declaring that all nations under his
> rule should "adhere to the religion taught by St. Peter to the
> Romans"; this was followed later by edicts against all heretics,
> depriving them of their churches. . . . With the conversion of the
> Empire the relationship between Church and State entered on a
> new phase." [1]

[1] Cyril Garbett, *Church and State in England* (London: Hodder & Stoughton, 1950), pp. 13-14. Used by permission of the publisher.

The word "conversion" in the last sentence of that quotation must be taken in a sense consistent with the fact that it was the Empire that was converted, not all the people in it. Its conversion consisted of making orthodox Christianity the only lawful or permitted religion. But even the Empire was not "converted" until two generations after the time of Constantine. Meanwhile the Church was free from persecution, and so were the followers of all other religions.

In the absence of any reliable statistics it has been estimated that Christians constituted between 5 and 10 per cent of the population of the Empire in Constantine's time. By the end of his reign in 337 they were undoubtedly a much larger proportion, though still a minority. Two causes promoted rapid increase in the number of Christians: freedom from persecution and the open favor of the emperor.

The edict was neutral in regard to all religions, but Constantine was not. His mother, Helena, was a Christian. He believed that he had seen a miraculous sign indicating that by alliance with Christ he would win his crucial battle for the throne—and he won it. The Empire had already lost its religious homogeneity and was a complex of minorities, for the pagans themselves were divided into many groups with varying degrees of traditional reverence and sophisticated skepticism toward the old gods and with no cohesion among themselves. Among all these religious minorities Christianity seemed to be the one with the greatest promise and power. He did not yet realize how serious were the actual or potential divisions among Christians—Donatists against Catholics, Arians against Athanasians—and these were to involve him in unexpected difficulties, but he was shrewd enough to see that he would gain by throwing his weight on the side of the Christians.

So, from motives doubtless both political and religious Constantine let the light of his imperial favor shine on the Christians while maintaining the principle of legal tolerance toward all religions. He did close some pagan temples, especially some rather decadent ones in the eastern provinces, and he built some churches. Notably he transferred his seat of government to the old Greek city of Byzantium, rebuilt it, renamed it after himself as Constantinople, and made it essentially a Christian city by erecting churches and virtually excluding pagan worship. Over the gateway of his new palace in that city he placed an inscription declaring that Christ had given him his victories. When the trinitarian controversy threatened to disrupt the Church, he called the first general council to meet at Nicaea, not far from his new capital, paid its expenses and presided at some of its sessions. Perhaps the farthest reach of Constantine's identification with the Christian cause was when, as reported by his biographer Eusebius, he said to an assembly of bishops: "You have been installed bishops for the inner affairs of the Church, but I have been installed bishop by God for its outer affairs." And as he saw it, "outer" included theology—the Trinity, Logos, and *homoousion*. That Constantine postponed baptism until he was on his deathbed was due to the then current belief that baptism was the only positive guarantee of forgiveness for all sins up to date, so there was some worldly wisdom in delaying it until the candidate was too far gone to have any remaining power or opportunity to sin. The delay therefore did not indicate any lack of commitment to the Christian faith.

Even before his edict of 313 Constantine had shown favor to Christians. He ordered the proconsul of Africa to return confiscated church property; he gave fifteen thousand pounds to Caecilian, bishop of Carthage, to distribute among the needy clergy of his diocese; he exempted the Christian clergy from liability for certain municipal taxes, though the pagan priests were still required to pay them.

For all this, Constantine did not persecute the pagans or attempt to enforce religious uniformity in his Empire. The contrary has sometimes been said. Bishop Eusebius, his friend and admirer, lived long enough after Constantine's death (in 337) to write a eulogistic *Life of Constantine* in which he set it down as an item in Constantine's favor that he suppressed pagan worship. The evidence is against the historical accuracy of this statement. It is known that pagan worship continued in Rome and at many places in the provinces. Doubtless the enforcement of general laws against it would have been difficult or impossible, but there is no record that any such laws or edicts existed. But whether or not Constantine suppressed pagan worship, the significant thing is that Eusebius said he did and that he said it in a eulogy addressed to Christian readers and designed to exalt its subject as the ideal Christian monarch. This reveals the state of the Christian mind twenty-five years after the edict which had released them from persecution. So rapid had been the change in the character and attitudes of the Church in one generation—that is, from the time when Lactantius wrote his book extolling toleration until Eusebius wrote the *Life*—that Eusebius could be sure Constantine's glory would be enhanced in the eyes of Christians by a report that he had persecuted the pagans. It is true, as Lietzmann says, that this work by Eusebius "constituted a single impassioned tribute to the ideal of a world-wide Christian monarchy." The first great revolution in the character of the Church had already begun in the minds of its leaders.

The historical reality soon caught up with Eusebius' flattering exaggeration. The groundwork had already been laid for the final step in the transformation of the unity of a fellowship of believers bound together by a common devotion to one Lord into the unity of a "world-wide Christian monarchy" welded together by the threats, the blows, and the favors of the civil power reinforcing the unities of doctrine and administration which the Church was hammering out for itself within its own structure. I shall return to speak of the unity of creed in connection with the Council of Nicaea and the Arian controversy, and of the institutional unity in connection with the rise of the papacy.

In approaching the concept of the Church as coextensive with the entire population and as having its unity, purity, and universality guaranteed by the coercive power of the government, the idea of the Church as a "new Israel" was very helpful. At the risk of some repetition this idea, which was introduced on an earlier page and in another connection, must again be mentioned as one of the things that theologians and ecclesiastics now found useful in rationalizing the changes through which the Church was passing, or rather in trying to show that the Church was not making any changes but was simply continuing the realization of a pattern which God himself had laid down in the days of Moses.

The first application of this "new Israel" idea was in adding sanction to the distinction between clergy and laity and to the recognition of a priestly quality in the clergy. This thought seems to have found its first distinct statement in Tertullian. It was developed further in the third century. Gieseler, certainly no recent authority but still a respectable one, was speaking of that century when he wrote:

As the prevailing desire was now to compare the Mosaic institution with the Christian, of which it was regarded as the type, and to trace out an analogy even in their individual features, the idea soon occurred to the mind, of comparing the Christian officers in the church with the Mosaic priesthood, and of giving them the very same titles (summus sacerdos, sacerdotes, Levitae). As a body, they were called, by way of eminence, [kleros, tou theou, of God; klerikoi]; among the Latins, ordo; in opposition to the [laos, plebs, laikoi].[2]

Such phrases as "new Israel" and "true Israel" had at first connoted the contrast between Christianity and Judaism rather than continuity of the institution or similarity in structure. Paul in the Epistle to the Galatians saw Christians as the true spiritual descendants of Abraham and the heirs of his promise because they had a faith like his, in contrast with the genealogical children of his grandson Jacob (that is, Israel), who had forfeited it by their unbelief. So there was now a new

[2] J. C. L. Gieseler, *Ecclesiastical History* (New York: Harper & Bros., 1849), I, 159.

"people of God" in place of Israel—a people spiritually akin to the faithful Abraham but owing nothing to lineal descent from Jacob and free from the Mosaic law. This new people of God was the Church, the fellowship of believers in Christ. If Jews entered into this fellowship—as Paul prayed that they all might and as some of them did—they entered it on no special terms because they were Jews, and they imposed upon the Church of Paul's time none of the special characteristics of Judaism. But as the Church in actual practice developed structures and procedures similar to those of Israel, it became useful both to explain and to justify them by turning the contrast into an analogy and then into an affirmation of continuity and identity. The ministry became a priesthood, and since the old Israel had a priesthood, it could be made to seem quite natural that the "new Israel" should have one. The religious life of Israel had an institutional solidarity based upon a centralized authority. The Church as the "new Israel" could justify its development in that direction and the final elevation of one bishop to a place of supremacy. Judaism was (and is) essentially a hereditary religion; Christianity essentially is not. Christianity is, of course, socially transmitted, and since the family is the most intimate and basic social group, the family is Christianity's most important channel of transmission from generation to generation, as it is for other social values. The analogy with Israel tended to emphasize and even to enforce this hereditary character. It came to be said, for example, that baptism "came in place of circumcision." The religion of Israel had been in principle and in practice the religion of the entire nation. Its law prescribed methods—and very rugged ones— for compelling conformity and insuring that membership of the "Jewish Church" (if that term can be legitimately used, which I doubt) should be coextensive with the entire body of the citizenship. Not long after the Christian Church was freed from persecution and began to enjoy the favor of the emperor, it began to adopt that same view of its relation to the social order and the same means of protecting its monopoly. The claim that the Church was the "new Israel" was a powerful argument in support of the claim that it was entitled to enjoy the same status and employ the same methods that the religion of the old Israel had enjoyed and employed in its nation.

(Parenthetically and as indicating how firmly this Israelitic idea became fixed in the mind of the Church, it may be noted that we find Governor Winthrop in Puritan colonial Massachusetts arguing that there should be no democracy in New England because there had been none in Israel.)

It is not suggested that this belated identification of the Church with Israel was the sole cause, or even the most important cause, of the radical change in the Church's character and in the nature of its unity that was now about to appear. Its significance was rather that in the fourth century it lent an apparently divine sanction to a new theory of the Church's relation to government and to the social order that was a novel factor then and a disastrous factor thereafter in Christian thought and practice for the next thousand years and more.

It was probably not more than ten years after the appearance of Eusebius' grateful, but mistaken, praise of Constantine for suppressing all non-Christian worship, and certainly not later than the middle of the fourth century, that the Christian theologian Julius Firmicus Maternus, a rather recent convert, was calling upon the succeeding emperors, Constans and Constantius, the two survivors among Constantine's four sons, to use the sword for the extermination of the pagans. In a book dedicated to the two emperors and entitled *De Errore Profanarum Religionum,* Maternus wrote:

Upon you, most sacred emperors, is laid the duty of punishing this crime [paganism], and this command is given to you by the command of the most high God, that your severity pursue this widespread villany. Hear and take to heart what God commands concerning this crime: "If thy brother, the son of thy mother, or thy son, or thy daughter, or the wife of thy bosom, or thy friend which is as thine own soul entice thee secretly, saying, Let us go and serve other gods which thou hast not known, thou nor thy fathers; namely, the gods of the peoples which are round about you, nigh unto thee or far off from thee, from the one end of the earth even unto the other end of the earth; thou shalt not consent unto him, nor harken unto him; neither shalt thine eye pity him, neither shalt thou spare, neither shalt thou conceal him: But thou shalt surely kill him; thine hand shall be the first upon him to put him to death, and afterwards the hand of all the people; And thou shalt stone him with stones that he die; because he hath sought to thrust thee away from the Lord thy God, which brought thee out of the land of Egypt, from the house of bondage" (Deut. 13:6-10). He commands that neither son nor brother be spared, and he makes the sword an avenger by the hand of a loved consort. He pursues a friend with extreme severity, and the whole population is armed to tear to pieces the bodies of the sacrilegious ones. Destruction is decreed for entire states if they should be found guilty of that crime. And that your majesties may learn this the more clearly, I will suggest the substance of an edict.[3]

This, I repeat, was scarcely half a century after Lactantius had been championing a policy of equal tolerance for all religions, and a scant generation after the edict of 313 had granted exactly that. The shocking contrast cannot be brushed off by saying, as Lietzmann does (*From Constantine to Julian*, p. 255), that Maternus was an "obscure person" and that "his polemic has the rather nasty flavor of a renegade fouling his former nest." To be sure, it has a "nasty flavor," but the policy he recommended was in substance that which much more eminent churchmen approved and the Christian emperors were beginning to put into practice within very few years, and he fouled his new Christian nest more than his old pagan one. Though extravagant and fanatical in its language, and perhaps without much actual influence on the course of events, it was precisely in line with the developments which the most eminent Christian leaders were soon promoting.

The legal steps which brought about this revolutionary

[3] Text quoted in *ibid.*, I, 274.

change need be mentioned only in bare outline. The important point is that they were all taken with the approval of the Church and most of them at its urgent demand. The sons of Constantine issued a decree in 341 ordering an "end of the folly of [pagan] sacrifices," but there is no record of its enforcement. In 350 Constantius decreed the death penalty for sacrificing to the pagan gods, but again enforcement was impossible. There were still too many pagans. In 353 the closing of pagan temples "in every place" was ordered, and sacrifices were forbidden, with a sliding scale of penalties. In 356 all "worshipers of idols" were threatened with the death penalty. Some temples were destroyed, and others were converted into churches, but the ancient rites continued in many places, even in Rome, where the pagan festivals were still observed. Constantius visited Rome only once in his entire reign, in 357. At that time he noted the general adherence of the nobility to paganism. He confirmed the privileges of the Vestal Virgins, observed with complacency the continued patronage of pagan shrines and altars, and granted public funds for the support of the pagan ritual. So wrote the prominent pagan senator Symmachus in 384.

Julian the Apostate attempted a revival of the old religion. As Constantine had been officially neutral while favoring Christianity, so Julian gave legal toleration to all religions but favored paganism. His reign of only two years, 361-63, imposed a brief check on the policy of suppressing non-Christians, and during nearly twenty years thereafter the imperial program was relatively tolerant. It was in this interval that the prefect of Rome replaced the images of the twelve gods at the edge of the Roman forum (in 367 or 368). Symmachus (c. 345-405) claimed to speak for a majority of the Senate in saying that the survival of Rome depended upon a return to the pagan faith. This was the view which Augustine combated a few years later in his *City of God,* when there still remained a sufficient pagan element to warrant such a formidable answer to the argument that the capture of Rome by Alaric the Goth was due to its abandonment of the old gods. While Bishop (pope) Damasus (366-84) was encouraging Jerome in his work on the Latin Vulgate, considerable numbers among the Roman aristocracy were worshipers of Mithra, and others were celebrating the Saturnalia while the Christians were celebrating Christmas.

The council of Constantinople (the second ecumenical) in 381 marked the beginning of a new campaign against paganism, and this campaign was stepped up and neared its climax when Theodosius became sole emperor in 392. As emperor in the East Theodosius had already encouraged the demolition of temples, forbidden even private pagan rites, and decreed that apostates from Christianity should be deprived of such civic rights as making wills or inheriting property. His ordinances were more strictly enforced in the East than in the West, but after he gained the full imperial power at the death of Valentinian II, the matter of tolerating paganism became a closed issue as it had never been before. While it still took some decades to effect its complete extinction, the advance in that direction was constant—and violent. Theodosius II (401-50) authorized a campaign which amounted almost to a crusade. The operations of the police power of the state were reinforced by mob action encouraged by leaders of the Church. Organized bands of monks ranged like "goon gangs" through many rural areas in the East burning temples and doing violence to their patrons, while proletarian Christian mobs did the same in the cities.

In the east, the Christians proceeded far beyond the imperial ordinances. Enterprising bishops led mobs of hirelings or fanatics against the temples; and the monks especially often combined for the destruction of all heathen sanctuaries. . . . The destruction of the splendid temple of Serapis 391 by the violent Theophilus, bishop of Alexandria, after a bloody contest, announced the total overthrow of paganism in the east. . . . Crowds of monks were sent about through the provinces with full power from the emperors, for the purpose of destroying all traces of idolatry. Even misdeeds and murders were allowed to pass unheeded by the emperors; such as the horrible murder of the female philosopher *Hypatia* in Alexandria (416). The new-platonic philosophers at Athens, and among them even the celebrated *Proclus* . . . , were forced to conceal themselves most carefully, because they rejected Christianity. As early as 423, all visible traces of paganism had disappeared in the east.[4]

The great Augustine—he of the *Confessions* and *The City of God*—gave the policy of persecution his personal approval and supplied a theological justification for it, though his concern was rather with heresy and schism than with paganism. It was at precisely this period that he wrote the words which will presently be quoted as a shining illustration of the revolution which had taken place in the mind and character of the Church. Pope Leo I (440-61) openly favored putting heretics to death, so it may be presumed that he would have dealt no more gently with pagans, but by his time they had been so nearly extinguished that they were less a problem to him than the heretics. Pockets of paganism did remain, however, in remote places. The word *pagani* to designate worshipers of the old gods was first officially used in an edict of Valentinian in 368, because even as early as that the old religion was supposed to have been pushed out into the villages and rural areas, though actually it was then probably stronger among the Roman aristocracy than anywhere else. "Pagan" meant peasant, just as the word "heathen," coming from Germanic sources, originally meant dwellers on the heath. Both words had something of the contemptuous connotation of "hillbilly." Even a century and a half after the time of Augustine and Leo I there seem to have been some remaining pagans in remote rustic regions, but Pope Gregory I (590-604) regarded them as no longer important enough to be worth dignifying by death. In one of his letters he advised in the case of any peasant who remains pagan in any of the outlying places (Sicily, Sar-

[4] *Ibid.*, I, 283, 284, 287-88.

dinia, or Corsica), if he stubbornly refuses to accept Christianity, "that he should be loaded with such a burden of taxes that the severity of the exaction shall force him to yield." [5]

By lack of fuel the fierce fires of persecution against pagans had burned themselves down to this feeble flicker. The whole population of the Empire was now "Christian." The Church of committed believers had now become a *Landeskirche* including everybody. Thoughtful men realized, however, even while approving the process of persecution as a means of consolidating the whole social order in one Church, that all might not be well with the state of religion. Jerome wrote: "We ought to be careful about those who become Christians not by choice but by compulsion, whose timid minds are swayed by fear of offending the rulers." [6] Augustine, thinking of those who accepted Christianity for social or political advantage after it became popular rather than of those who were driven into it by threat of death, wrote:

How many seek Jesus only in order that he may bring them some temporal advantage! One has a business matter in which he wants the intervention of the clergy; another, under pressure from someone more powerful than himself, flees to the church; another wants help against someone with whom he is too weak to cope; one for one such reason, another for another. Daily the church is being filled with such. Scarcely ever is Jesus sought for his own sake. [7]

Thus far I have spoken only of the conflict between Christianity and paganism, and of Christianity's victory when the emperors declared in its favor and made it the official religion of the Empire. The Roman state had always considered that it had the right and duty to exercise some degree of control over the religion of its people by enforcing at least a minimum

[5] *Epistolae*, Bk. IV, ep. 26.
[6] *Commentary on Isaiah*, 60:14.
[7] *Tractate on the Gospel of John* 21:10.

of common cultus sufficient to serve as a unifying factor in its vast and diversified domain. A single century, the fourth, had exhibited the following successive phases:

1. The state persecutes the Church in order to enforce conformity to its traditional pagan patterns; the Church, still an entirely voluntary fellowship of believers, asks religious liberty for itself and for all religions, and defends its unity by declaring that heretics and schismatics are no part of it.

2. The state grants full liberty to all religions; the Church gladly accepts this liberty.

3. The Church begins to demand the suppression of its rival, paganism; the state for a time stands by its policy of official neutrality between these two, even while backing one party within the Church against the other—for example, Athanasians versus Arians, or vice versa.

4. The state yields to the Church's demand for the extermination of paganism, and thus the state comes back in principle to the point from which it started, that is, the policy of seeking spiritual and cultural unity by the enforcement of a single religion on all its citizens, but now the enforced religion is Christianity instead of paganism and emperor worship. The Church has now completely changed its character from voluntary to compulsory; it accepts the idea, at once pagan Roman and Hebraic, of a single permitted religion in a governmental or national area, and Church and state together commit themselves unreservedly to the theory that, unless Christianity is the religion of all the people in the Empire, the state will totter and all the bonds of the social order will be dissolved.

There was, however, another conflict, no less bitter than that between Christianity and paganism, which must be resolved if the Church was to enjoy its victory and maintain its unity and if the state was to find in Christianity the stabilizing and unifying influence which it had expected. That was the conflict, or series of conflicts, within the Church itself. These conflicts were precipitated by two related but clearly distinguishable things which came to be called "heresy" and "schism." Both are

101

partisan terms, loaded with prejudicial connotations, but we must use them because there are no single words by which to denote the events to which they were applied except these that were coined by the "Catholic" party which ultimately became dominant. Both types of dissent threatened the unity of the Church. Heresy threatened the unity of its doctrine; schism, the unity of its structure.

The term "Catholic" seems to have appeared first in the writings of Ignatius, who according to some scholars died in A.D. 107, in his *Epistle to Smyrna* (ch. 8) in the sense of the Church universal as distinguished from local. In the *Martyrdom of Polycarp* (sec. 16, A.D. 155) it means orthodox in contrast with heretical. The word is also found in the Muratorian Fragment (A.D. 190) and in Clement of Alexandria (d. 217). Even before the end of the second century critical pagans were bringing against Christianity the reproach—often heard today —that it was divided into so many sects that the only sensible thing was to reject them all. To this objection Clement, who lived in the world's greatest hotbed of heresies and isms, replied that Judaism also had its sects and Greek philosophy its schools of thought, and that only a fool would refuse to call a doctor because there were several schools of medicine. But Clement was more complacent than most in regard to diversity of doctrine within the one Church, perhaps because he himself had a tinge of Gnosticism. Clement of Alexandria was for many centuries regarded as a Roman Catholic saint and had a day (December 4) in the Roman calendar, but Pope Clement VIII—the same who had Giordano Bruno burned in 1600—ordered his name stricken from the list.

Irenaeus, who died about A.D. 202, has been called the "father of orthodoxy." C. C. Crutwell in *A Literary History of Early Christianity* (p. 374) says that to him "belongs the distinction of stereotyping the genius of orthodoxy and founding the Church's polemic method." His determination was to maintain the "apostolic tradition" unchanged as against the current welter of "heretical" speculations and opinions. It did not occur

to him or to his like-minded contemporaries that, in combating
variant opinions on questions about which the apostles had
said nothing, they were forced to expand the apostolic tradition by including in it not only what the apostles had said
and written but also what the orthodox believed the apostles
would have said and written if these questions had been raised
in their time. Consequently it did not seem to them that they
were doing anything other than defending the truth against
insidious forms of error when they created doctrinal conditions of Christian fellowship which were unknown in the age
of the apostles. The consolidation of the Church's doctrinal
position and the place of Irenaeus in that movement are thus
noted by Edgar J. Goodspeed:

Toward A.D. 180 Christian leaders, hard pressed after half a
century of schismatic movements, Docetic, Gnostic, and Marcionite,
by the extravagant claims and eccentric activities of the Montanist
sect, . . . agreed to organize the scattered churches into one General, or Catholic, church, to maintain a standard type of Christianity. The idea was as old as Ephesians, but its practical application to the problem of the perplexed and harassed churches had
not been made before. Of this new movement, fraught with such
significance, our first reflections are in the writings of Irenaeus.[8]

As has already been said, Irenaeus urged that real heretics
be cut off from the Church, but there were limits to the degree
of standardization by exclusion that he could countenance.
When Victor, bishop of Rome (about A.D. 190), assumed the
right to excommunicate all the Eastern churches because they
would not accept the method of determining the date of Easter
that he and the Western churches favored, Irenaeus protested
in the name of liberty and unity, though he himself was of the
West (bishop of Lyons) and preferred the Western method.
On matters of doctrine, however, he was adamant and could

[8] *A History of Early Christian Literature* (University of Chicago Press, 1942),
p. 193.

103

find no room in the Church for differences of opinion. Polycarp had called Marcion "the first-born of Satan, ˙ and Irenaeus at the end of the second century and Tertullian early in the third would doubtless have regarded the "heretics" of their time as being of the same lineage and thus as having no place whatever in the Church.

As the Church moved into the crucial fourth century, it found the problem of its heretics and schismatics growing even more serious, but now it had a new resource for dealing with them and for preserving its unity in spite of them. It had the government. The unity it was now set to maintain and defend was a unity of structure (in so far as this had been attained) and a unity of doctrine. The first of these was most formidably threatened by the Donatist schism; the second, by the Arian heresy. Donatism, though mildly heretical at a few points and tending to become more so, was primarily a schism because it definitely seceded from the organized main body in North Africa (A.D. 316) and organized its own corps of bishops and its own system of discipline. Arianism was primarily a heresy rather than a schism because its objective was to remain in the recognized structure of the Church and to make its distinctive doctrine the doctrine of the Catholic Church.

Fortunately it is not essential for our present purpose to trace the intricate ramifications of this struggle. Our concern in this book is with concepts of the nature of the Church's unity and with the means adopted for its attainment and preservation. Obviously the Church would not be an effective influence in unifying the already shattered and dissolving empire unless it was itself united. Just as obviously the Church could not maintain its claim to catholicity—that is, universality—by continuing forever its earlier policy of simply excommunicating the heretics and letting the schismatics go their way in peace. State and Church had a common interest in using whatever measures might be necessary to whip the dissenters and separatists into line, just as they were at the same

time doing to suppress paganism and put the Church in undisputed possession of the whole field.

The Donatist controversy, beginning even before the edict
of toleration, grew out of a demand by Donatus and many
north African bishops for a stricter policy in regard to ab-
solving and readmitting to the Church those who had weakened
under persecution and denied the faith. They and their followers also revived the rather extravagant claims of the earlier
Montanists as to the possession of "spiritual gifts." As always,
the Spirit-filled enthusiasts were impatient of control by those
whom they considered merely officeholding ecclesiastics, however authentically ordained and consecrated, and they could
not regard as properly Christian the unconverted multitudes
that were pouring into the Church as membership in it was
coming to be a social and political asset.

An appeal was made to Constantine in a quarrel at Carthage
which presaged the beginning of serious hostilities between
Donatists and Catholics. By his order a synod or royal commission attended by bishops from Gaul, Italy, and Africa met
at Rome in September, 313. The African delegation consisted
of ten bishops from each party. The decision was against the
Donatists, but this was only the beginning of the struggle.
Another meeting was held at Carthage, and the next year another at Arles in Gaul with bishops in attendance from many
places from Britain to Dalmatia. The result was the same.
Constantine issued an edict (date unknown) confiscating
Donatist churches but later rescinded it and apparently decided
that, since this schism was confined to North Africa, he could
safely leave it to burn itself out. Instead, it blazed up more
fiercely long after his time and seems to have come near to
taking North Africa. In 411 a great council was held at Carthage with more than one hundred bishops of each party
present. Neither arguments nor negotiations met with any success. Whether or not Donatism would have died a natural
death in time, as seems not unlikely, it was not allowed to do

so. The power of the state was invoked, and Donatism was extinguished by military action.

The Donatist threat was at its height when Augustine was bishop of Hippo, on the North African coast. Paganism was already under the ban before Augustine became influential as a Christian. (He was baptized in 387, became a bishop in 391; the decisive edict of Theodosius banning paganism was in 392.) The policy of both Church and state in dealing with paganism was well established and in such successful operation that the attainment of its objective was no longer doubtful. But what should be the policy toward heretical and schismatic Christians? That was not exactly a new question either. The ebb and flow of imperial favor and popular opinion on Arianism and Athanasianism had given occasion for intervention by the state, now on one side, now on the other, but the punishment was usually removal from office or banishment or both. The death penalty for heresy was first inflicted in 385, and Arianism was not the issue in this case. The victim was Priscillian, a Spanish ascetic who had become bishop of Avila. He was a premature advocate of clerical celibacy and went so far as to recommend celibacy even to lay Christians who wished to be "perfect." He was burned alive at Treves with six of his companions. The state took the initiative in this drastic action, but a church synod at Treves immediately voted its approval. Ambrose of Milan and Martin of Tours protested against such severity and succeeded in checking the persecution of the Priscillianists. Augustine, I think, would not have approved of the burning of heretics as a regular practice, though he must bear a share of the responsibility for its becoming that.

When it came to dealing with the troublesome Donatists, Augustine was heartily in favor of giving them the kind of treatment they actually got. They were a turbulent and intractable element in the region for which he felt special responsibility. Their demand for an impossible standard of purity and their resistance to the constituted authorities were dividing the Church. The great debate with a hundred bishops on each side had produced no conversions either way. Reasoning and persuasion seemed to produce no beneficial effect. When the imperial troops were called in to clean up the situation, Augustine was heartily glad of it. The tremendous prestige of Augustine and the unparalleled influence which he exercised over the thinking and the policies of the Church for many centuries after his own time justify taking a little space to make his record on this matter perfectly clear, and in his own words.

Augustine's commitment to the technique of compulsory orthodoxy and the liquidation of heretics is most clearly stated in a letter which he wrote in reply to one that he believed Vincentius of Lérins had written protesting against the use of violence to put down heresy. (On all other points Vincentius was known to be perfectly orthodox. It was he who coined the famous criterion of orthodoxy—*quod ubique, quod semper, quod ab omnibus creditum est.*) It appeared later that Vincentius did not write the letter which Augustine answered, but it served just as well to give the bishop of Hippo occasion to set down in black and white his argument in defense of persecution as a method of making the true faith prevail. There had been a time, wrote Augustine, when he himself thought that only argument and persuasion ought to be used with heretics, but the logic of events had convinced him of the contrary. He had tried persuasion on the Donatists. It did not work, and violence did. The fact that many cities once defiantly Donatist are now soundly Catholic is proof enough that the method used in their conversion was a good method. This purely pragmatic argument, however, could be reinforced by a rational argument. Augustine continues:

If we were to overlook and forbear with these cruel enemies who so disturb our peace and quietness by manifold and grievous forms of violence and treachery [the Donatists were not, in fact, any more violent and treacherous than the Catholics, but this was a way of describing "heretics"], so that nothing at all should be contrived or done by us with a view to alarm or correct them, truly we would be rendering evil for evil. For if anyone saw his enemy running headlong to destroy himself when he had become delirious through a dangerous fever, would he not in that case be much more rendering evil for evil if he permitted him to run on thus than if he took measures to have him seized and bound? . . .

You will say that to some these remedies are of no service. Is the art of healing therefore to be abandoned because the malady of some is incurable? You look only to the case of those who are so obdurate that they refuse even such correction. Of such it is written: "In vain have I smitten your children; they received no correction" (Jer. 2:30). And yet I suppose that those of whom the prophet speaks were smitten in love, not from hatred. But you ought to consider also the very large number over whose salvation we rejoice. For if they were only made afraid and were not instructed, this might appear to be a kind of inexcusable tyranny. Again, if they were instructed only and not made afraid, they would be with more difficulty persuaded to embrace the way of salvation. . . .

You are of opinion that no one should be compelled to follow righteousness; and yet you read that the householder said to his servants: "Whomsoever ye shall find, compel them to come in." . . . You are of opinion also that no coercion is to be used with any man in order to his deliverance from the fatal consequences of error; and yet you see that, in examples that cannot be disputed, this is done by God.

You now see therefore, I suppose, that the thing to be considered when anyone is coerced is not the mere fact of the coercion, but the nature of that to which he is coerced, whether it be good or bad.

In this final sentence Augustine strikes the note which is characteristic of all defenses of religious intolerance or of special privileges for one form of religion over another. *"Our religion should have special status and privileges because it is right."* "Error has not the same rights as truth—and we have the truth." "Heresy (to be defined by us) is a spiritual pestilence that must be quarantined and eradicated." "Schismatics and dissenters are madmen rushing to their own destruction

108

and creating a public peril, so they must be restrained for their own good or put out of the way for the common welfare." From this avowed doctrine of intolerance, fortified by the conviction that the state cannot stand unless its citizens are united in one religion and that a church cannot be respected unless the entire body of society is in one way or another brought into its membership, it followed as a necessary corollary that the power of the state may legitimately be invoked— indeed, *must* be invoked—to insure universal adherence, or submission, to the religion with which the state had allied itself. From the Christian standpoint not just any religion could serve as the cement of the social order. Augustine elaborated an argument which may be summarized in this: no commonwealth without justice, no justice without true virtue, no virtue without the true religion.[9]

Augustine sought scriptural sanction for an all-inclusive church membership by citing: the comparison of the Church to a net which catches all kinds of fish; Jesus' choice of Judas to "furnish His Church an example of bearing with the wicked"; the injunction to "go out into the highways and byways and compel them to come in"; and the parable of the tares (Matt. 13:24-30) —not including verse 36, which says that the "field is the world," not the Church.[10] Like Eusebius, and perhaps relying on his authority, he reported with approval, but erroneously, that Constantine ordered the "idols of the Gentiles everywhere . . . to be overthrown." [11]

By the year 450 Donatism was virtually extinct. Only a little more than two centuries later the westward sweep of Islam obliterated Catholic Christianity in North Africa by methods not different in principle from those which Augustine had recommended in dealing with its rival.

The most serious threat to the doctrinal unity of the Church grew out of the theological differences which the Council of

[9] *The City of God,* Bk. XIX, chs. 17, 21, 24.
[10] *Ibid.,* Bk. XVIII, ch. 49.
[11] *Ibid.,* Bk. V, ch. 26.

Nicaea (325) undertook to settle. The important issue was as to the metaphysical nature of Christ, or one might say that it concerned the inner structure of the Godhead. No one was saying that Jesus was a "mere man," or simply a uniquely inspired prophet, or even, as a Gnostic might have said, that he possessed a lower order of divinity than God the Father. All agreed that Christ was a pre-existent being through whom all things had been created. The dispute hinged upon more subtle distinctions than that between divinity and humanity. The conflict broke out in Alexandria, where Arius, an elderly presbyter of the church in that city, was shocked to hear his bishop declare that Christ was coeternal with the Father, that he was the "ever-begotten" or the "unbegotten-begotten." This seemed to him to compromise the unity of God. His view was that Christ was the first of created beings and that God the Father had given him a substance like his own. From the scanty unbiased evidence—for the accounts of the position of Arius come chiefly from his enemies—it seems that he regarded the term "Son" as used in a figurative sense in the Scriptures and the word "begotten" as an objectionably literalistic extension of the implications of that figure. The protagonist of the other opinion was Athanasius, a young archdeacon of the same church and soon its bishop, at thirty-three, five months after the close of the Nicene Council. He held to the equality, the coeternity, and the substantial identity of the Father and the Son, though the Father is still distinctively the Father and the Son the Son while both, together with the Holy Spirit, are one God.

The struggle which had broken out at Alexandria spread quickly all over the East. Constantine undertook to settle it by a wave of the imperial hand, not by exercising arbitrary power but by urging the contending parties to get together and settle their differences, which did not seem to him to be serious. He called a council in A.D. 325 at Nicaea, not far from his new capital at Constantinople, paid the traveling expenses of those who attended, and presided at some of the sessions. This was the first "general" council of the Church, though only two or three churchmen from west of the Adriatic were present. Constantine's friend and technical adviser on church affairs, Eusebius, submitted to the council the draft of a creed couched chiefly in biblical language which he thought everyone could sign and thus restore the unity of the Church. But the Athanasian party wanted a creed that the Arians could not sign, so that the unity of the Church could be restored by casting them out as heretics. After stormy sessions the council hit upon the word *homoousion,* "of the same substance," as the best description of the metaphysical (though not personal) identity of Christ with the Father. Only the pressure applied by Constantine brought this theological victory. The word is said to have been coined for the purpose of Hosius, bishop of Cordova. Athanasius himself seldom used it in his subsequent writings, but it became the touchstone of orthodoxy. Its opposite, favored by the Arians, was *homoiousion,* "of similar substance."

The years following Nicaea were turbulent ones for the Church and for all the persons who had been taking leading parts in the struggle. First Arius was condemned and exiled. Later he persuaded Constantine that he was orthodox enough and that he had been abused by designing and unscrupulous enemies. Arius was recalled, and Athanasius was banished, though not on theological grounds. Later Athanasius was restored to his see. The struggle raged, with fluctuating fortunes, throughout his long life and much later. At times there appeared to be an even chance that Arianism would triumph and become the "orthodox" Christian doctrine. The stronger it became, the more bitter grew the hostility between the parties and the more completely convinced did the Athanasian party become that its rival, and indeed all heresy, must be suppressed by whatever governmental power it could summon. The Arian sympathies of some of the emperors after Constantine and the paganism of Julian hindered the execution of this program, but caused no abandonment of the principle, now

111

firmly established, that it was the business of the state to support the true Catholic religion and suppress all variations in doctrine or practice, and thus to maintain the unity of the Church.

If it was essential to the health and unity of the Church that the structure of the Trinity be correctly defined in terms unknown to Scripture, and if *homoousion* was the indispensable word to give due honor to Christ and describe the relation of his "substance" to that of the Father, then indeed Arianism was a serious threat. It was widely accepted in the East. A synod in Seleucia in 360, a full generation after Nicaea, rejected both *homo-* and *homoi-ousion* as contrary to Scripture. Ulfilas, the missionary to the Goths, converted that aggressive nation of "barbarians" to Arian Christianity. Alaric's Goths who captured Rome in 410, and thereby stirred Augustine to write *The City of God,* were Arian Christians. Theodoric, who founded the Ostrogothic kingdom of Italy and ruled it for nearly forty years until 526, was an Arian, and his enlightened administration did credit of the cause. The Visigoths carried Arianism into Spain. On the other hand, synods at Arles (353) and Milan (355) required all bishops to subscribe the condemnation of Arius, and any who refused were deposed by the Church and banished by the civil power. The main strength of the Empire, so long as the Empire had any strength, was enlisted on the "Catholic" side. What S. L. Greenslade says about the crushing of the Donatists is equally true, as he indicates, of the compulsion which the government brought to bear against the Arians:

With the accession of Gratian and later of Theodosius, emperors who openly set themselves to establish the orthodox and catholic Church, the Donatists were exposed both to measures expressly directed against them and also to the general laws against heretics. ... In 376 Gratian ordered the confiscation of heretical meeting-houses and threatened magistrates who tolerated illegal assemblies. In the next year another edict confirmed those of 373 and 376, and so it went on, almost every year seeing some measure against heresy. Some proscribed heresy in general, or heretical assemblies; others defined the catholic communion by reference to named orthodox bishops. One, in 386, assimilated the offense of troubling the peace of the Church to treason, thus making it nominally a capital crime; another, in 388, made the public discussion of religion punishable by death. Several of these constitutions were little more than pious aspirations, declarations of what the emperors approved and desired rather than of what they intended to enforce rigorously. The law of 392, which imposed a fine of ten pounds weight of gold upon heretical clergy, was more terrifying because more likely to be applied. . . .

From general toleration in 313 we have passed to the proscription of pagan worship and of heresy in 392; and by 425 the word *schismatici* was added to *haeretici* in relevant legislation.[12]

Nothing would be gained for the purposes of this book by undertaking even a brief recital of the historical events in and through which the Church carried out this policy of enforced unity in faith and practice throughout the entire medieval period. The old Roman Empire dissolved, and a new empire arose, built upon the ruins of the old by the fresh forces of peoples who had been barbarians when Rome was in her prime. The principles and policies which had been established during the decline and fall of the Roman Empire, and during the consolidation of the Church in government and doctrine, carried over into and through the Middle Ages.

Medieval thought was dominated by the idea of hierarchy, if that word is taken not in its original sense as meaning rule by priests but as describing a closely integrated and tightly woven system of graduated powers and dignities with the common man at the bottom, God at the top, the various ranks of civil and ecclesiastical authorities in an ascending scale between. In this "pyramid to God" every individual had his place in strict subordination to those above him and in author-

---

[12] *Schism in the Early Church* (London: Student Christian Movement Press, and New York: Harper & Bros., 1953), pp. 137, 142. Used by permission of S. C. M. Press.

ity over those below him. The two visible and concrete embodiments of this pattern were the Church and the feudal empire. The actual world never quite perfectly conformed to the ideal pattern. The feudal system, under which every man was to be knitted into the fabric of society by a method of government and land tenure and a gradation of status which determined all his rights and duties, began to break up before it was universally put into practice. The growth of the cities, the changing economic and industrial order, and the rise of nationalism all tended toward the disintegration of the system on its secular side. Antiecclesiastical schisms and heresies which rebelled against control from Rome, independent evangelical movements that went back to Scripture as the source of religious truth, mystics who sought direct access to God, free thinkers who relied upon the truth-finding power of the individual intellect—all these threatened to disturb the symmetry and stability of the "pyramid" as a system of total control in the realm of religion, and they must therefore be dealt with by whatever means might be necessary in order to extinguish them or render them harmless.

To appreciate the beauty and grandeur of the medieval concept and give to what one must call its intolerance a proper setting against the background of a great conviction, one must grasp the meaning and majesty of this design for an ideal unity of the world. Much later, science brought the idea of a universal reign of law in the natural world. Newton found the apple and the moon obeying the same law of falling bodies. The modern scientific mind seeks to picture the universe as integrated in one great system. The medieval unity was of a different order. It was personal and institutional both in the ground of its authority and in the agencies through which control was exercised. Not being interested in the uniformity of natural law, it left ample room for supernatural events. Indeed, supernaturalism was of the essence of it. Under the supernatural authority which it conceived as dominating the whole, its human world was ordered and unified by the opera-

114

tion of a hierarchy of authorities. Rebellion against that system was heresy, blasphemy, anarchy, and treason. It was not merely dissent or defection from Church or state; it was revolt against the fundamental constitution of things—against God. It was like the revolt of Lucifer against the King of Heaven. Medieval intolerance must be viewed in the light of this conviction that the hierarchy of authorities, constituting the "pyramid to God," was the essential order of human society in conformity with divine law. The elimination of discordant elements was essential to the protection of that system. Of that system the unity of the Church was the very heart and core. And in this context "Church" means a visible, organized structure.

One of the most universally respected of modern Roman Catholic theologians correctly points out that the persecution of heretics has not been a distinctively Catholic practice:

It is true that heretics were tried and burnt in the Middle Ages. But that was not done only in Catholic countries, for Calvin himself had Servetus burnt. And capital punishment was employed against the Anabaptists, especially in Thuringia and in the Electorate of Saxony. According to the Protestant theologian, Walter Köhler, even Luther after 1530 regarded the penalty of death as a justifiable punishment for heresy. The fact that the persecution of heresy was approved as a justifiable thing by non-Catholic bodies, and in certain cases carried out in practice, goes to show that such persecution did not spring from the nature of Catholicism, or in particular from its exclusive claims. The origin of such persecutions is to be sought rather in the Byzantine and medieval conception of the state, whereby every attack on the unity of the faith was regarded as an open crime against the unity and stability of the state, and one which had to be punished according to the primitive methods of the time.[13]

It is well to remember that the issue in regard to the employment of persecution as a means of maintaining the unity

[13] Karl Adam, *The Spirit of Catholicism* (rev. ed.; New York: The Macmillan Co., 1940), p. 198. Copyright 1940. Used by permission of the publisher.

of the Church, either as a whole or in a given area, is not an issue between Protestants and Catholics. In the next chapter we shall consider how the great Reformation churches took over the basic concepts which had long been almost universally accepted and used them to the extent of their opportunities. However, some reservations must be made while giving general approval to the substance of Karl Adam's paragraph. First, persecution of heretics originated quite as much from a conception of the Church as from a conception of the state, and it was the Church which took the initiative in demanding it. Second, its origin in the fourth century was much too early to be called "medieval," and its earlier and more drastic practice in the West than in the East forbids ascribing to it a "Byzantine" motivation. Surely the burning of a Spanish bishop in 385 for his views on Christian celibacy cannot be attributed to "Byzantine and medieval" statecraft. Third, the medieval conception of the state, when it did arrive later, and the "primitive methods of the time" were chiefly determined by the Church. Fourth, Luther and Calvin came a little late to be cited as examples of "medieval" intolerance or to have had anything to do with originating it.

We are not concerned about apportioning the responsibility for originating and maintaining the idea that the honor of the Church and the stability of the state alike demand a uniformity of religion in a united Church which can be protected only by the violent suppression of dissent. The historical fact is that, so far as concerns Christianity in the Roman Empire, this idea arose in the fourth century, was consistently applied in practice from that time until the Reformation in the sixteenth century, and was continued in varying degrees both in Protestant and Catholic countries until near the end of the seventeenth. An essential factor in this pattern of thought was a definite concept of what it meant for the Church to be united. It meant to have (1) a substantial body of theological doctrine formulated in a creed, approved by the highest ec-

116

clesiastical authority, and accepted by all, and (2) a unified governing body, or centralized control, for the Church.

Both of these conditions were approximated in the third century when the "Catholic" bishops were clearly distinguishable from other claimants and when their consensus had already established the main lines of orthodox doctrine. But as yet they could defend the "unity" of the Church on these terms only by casting out discordant elements. With the gaining of imperial favor, and then an exclusive status as the one legal religion, Catholic Christianity stabilized its unity by (1) the Nicene Creed, and (2) the development of the previously limited primacy of the bishop of Rome into what can now properly be called the papacy, with Leo I (440-61) if not earlier. Hierarchical unity was of slow and complicated growth, with much imperial and other political interference. It proceeded simultaneously with the widening cleavage between East and West in both governmental and ecclesiastical affairs and in the total cultures of these two divisions of what had been the Roman Empire. By the time of the Council of Chalcedon (451) there were four patriarchates in the East— Constantinople, Alexandria, Antioch, and Jerusalem. The bishops of Ephesus and Caesarea had been given a status between that of patriarch and metropolitan. Chalcedon decreed the equality of Constantinople and Rome, but Rome was unique in the West and its primacy there was unchallenged.

In 445 a law of Valentinian III declared the bishop of Rome to be supreme head of the western church because of the dignity of the city of Rome, the primacy of Peter, and the decree of a holy synod, and defined resistance to the bishop of Rome to be a crime against the Roman state. But meanwhile—as suggested by that limitation of primacy to the "western" church —the rift had already appeared which was to separate the churches east of the Adriatic from the Roman allegiance unto this day. This division was of profound importance. That it receives such scanty attention in this book is due only to our concentration upon a single line of development. Though the eastern church had a very different history and a different relation with the state, it gave expression in its own way to the same concept of the unity of the Church as requiring both doctrinal uniformity and subordination to centralized authorities, though not to a single authority comparable to the pope.

In recapitulation of this chapter let us note the changes through which the Church and state had passed from Constantine to the Reformation:

1. The Church of Constantine's day was still a voluntary society, as it had been from the beginning, but it had developed an extensive and fairly well-integrated episcopal polity, deferential but not obsequious toward Rome, and a substantial body of doctrine based upon the consensus of its principal bishops. It was free from the threat of persecution and had equal liberty along with all other forms of religion but was personally favored by the emperor. The Empire, accepting the Christian argument for general religious liberty, had abandoned its ancient demand for religious unity as essential to the stability of the state.

2. The Church consolidated both its doctrinal position by the Council at Nicaea and its polity by the elevation of the bishop of Rome to a position of unchallenged primacy. As the cleavage between East and West widened and deepened, and as the West submitted to papal absolutism, the Catholic Church in the West became the Roman Catholic Church.

3. Simultaneously the Church abandoned the voluntary principle and demanded that its status as the sole religion in the Empire be made secure by the forcible suppression of paganism and by the liquidation of heretics.

4. The state reverted to its former belief that religious homogeneity was essential to political stability, but now with Christianity instead of paganism as its one religion.

The resultant of these developments was the medieval

Church-and-state system. Conceiving its unity in terms of doctrine and structure, the Church west of the Adriatic remained united on this basis for more than a thousand years, but only by utilizing the police power of the state to reinforce the spiritual and temporal penalties that were at its command.

Chapter V

Classical Protestantism
NEW WINE IN OLD BOTTLES

THE PURPOSE OF THIS CHAPTER IS TO INDICATE THE WAYS IN which the principal Protestant churches in the period of the Reformation and for a considerable time thereafter carried over the medieval Roman Catholic ideas of the character of the visible Church, the nature of its unity, and the means by which its unity must be maintained, and to provide some documentation which will illustrate both the extent and the limits of this borrowing.

The term "classical Protestantism" in this context means the great Reformation churches of the sixteenth century with their direct prolongations into more modern times. These were the Lutheran, the Reformed (or Presbyterian), and the Anglican churches. These were all "national" churches, or *Landeskirchen*—that is, churches that were declared to be the official and sole churches of the political areas of their respective dominance. In this important respect these great churches of the Reformation period adopted and perpetuated the principles, the character, and to some extent the procedures of the medieval Church. There were, of course, some still more important departures from the medieval pattern. If there had not been, the Reformation would have amounted to nothing but a fragmentation of the Church, and it cannot be truthfully described in any such terms. But the high value that one may place upon the total movement of the Protestant Reformation and the grateful esteem in which one may rightly hold the heroic leaders of that movement must not be permitted to obscure the fact that, so far as concerns the nature of the Church's unity and the means of maintaining it, classical Protestantism differed from medieval Catholicism chiefly in the smaller scale on which it applied identical principles.

Under the medieval system the membership of the Church was held to be necessarily coextensive with the total population of the civilized world—or, in practice, of that portion of it west of the Adriatic, since the rift between East and West which was faintly visible in the fourth century had become an unbridgeable chasm by the eleventh. Its unity was a unity of dogma and structure, enforced by the compulsive power of both civil and ecclesiastical authorities. Sometimes these authorities did not act in harmony, or one of them frustrated the coercive efforts of the other. This was the situation which enabled Wycliffe to do his reformatory work in England and to die peacefully in bed. More frequently they collaborated efficiently, as when the Albigenses in southern France were exterminated in a crusade initiated and blessed by the Church and carried out by French troops, and when John Huss was burned at the Council of Constance by order of the Emperor Sigismund at the behest of the council, or when the Roman and Spanish inquisitions were doing their long continued deadly work.

The practicability of this method of maintaining this kind of unity in an all-inclusive Church was dependent upon the existence of an equally all-inclusive political power willing and able to implement the edicts of the Church for the suppression of schism, heresy, and dissent. Pope Boniface VIII stated the matter very clearly in his bull *Unam Sanctam* (1302):

We learn from the words of the Gospel that in this Church and in her power are two swords, the spiritual and the temporal. He who denies that the temporal sword is in the power of Peter, misunderstands the words of the Lord, "Put up thy sword into the sheath." Both are in the power of the Church, the spiritual sword and the material. But the latter is to be used *for* the Church, the former *by* her; the former by the priest, the latter by kings and captains but at the will and by the permission of the priest.

The "kings and captains" never accepted wholly or unanimously this simple definition of the relation of the temporal to the priestly power as one of complete subordination; and if all popes, including Boniface, had not subsequently been declared to be ex officio infallible, one might doubt whether even the Church continued to believe it. But it was accurate enough as indicating the function assigned to the state, and in general accepted by the state, in applying sufficient police pressure to insure the doctrinal purity, the structural solidity, and the universal spiritual empire of the Church dominated by the see of Rome.

The Protestant movement of the sixteenth century came at a time when this condition was no longer fulfilled. The Empire was breaking up. It had never had any effective apparatus of government. Some of its larger constituent elements, such as France, Spain, and England, had already become independent nations. Some of the smaller ones, notably the scores of feudal principalities in Germany, had gained such a degree of autonomy that they could not be relied upon to execute orders from the superior authorities. If the Church was to maintain its universal sway, and so its unity of the kind already described, it must now make its arrangements not with one wielder of the temporal sword (and it had never been quite that simple), but with many. And as it turned out, many of these independent political units sided with the Reform when the issue was raised and gave it areas of safety in which to gain its strength.

In a recent unpublished essay a scholarly author says: "The Protestant Reformation ultimately broke the unity of Western Christendom, and nationalism triumphed." The causal order of these events is rather the reverse of this if the reference is to the political unity of Western Christendom. It was the previous triumph of nationalism—and in some cases of regional autonomies that had not yet coalesced into nations—that made possible the kind of success the Protestant Reformation achieved. It was because Saxony, Hesse, Geneva, the Low Countries, Scotland, and England had already become autonomous jurisdictions not amenable to the authority of either emperor or pope, that the Protestant movements in these places were able to survive and to build their own exclusive jurisdictions in their respective areas. The ways in which the great Protestant churches made themselves safe and strong and tried to keep themselves united did not differ greatly from the ways in which the Roman Catholic Church had for more than a thousand years been making itself safe and strong and had been trying more or less successfully through those years to keep itself united.

The concept of the Church as expressed by Luther, Calvin, and the Protestant reformers who were their contemporaries differed from that of medieval and modern Roman Catholicism in the distinction it made between the Church invisible and the Church visible. This distinction made it possible for them to break with the visible structure having its seat of authority at Rome and still to maintain that they were in no way departing from the Church but were indeed liberating it from bondage to a usurping organization and giving it a visible form which would express its true character. Their formal definitions of the Church had reference to the true Church which, being spiritual and therefore invisible, consisted of all true believers and of them alone—or, as they sometimes put it, of all those whom God had elected to salvation and only of these—and only God could know exactly who these were. But for edification, for administration, for discipline, it was necessary that there should also be a Church visible. This could not be other than an *ecclesia mixta,* a field in which the true seed of the Word had been planted but in which the wheat and the tares must grow together until the Master of the harvest separated them. This visible Church must exist in territorial units. The nurture and administration of each of these units was the joint responsibility of its church organization and the civil magistrates of the area. The "tares" that were to be permitted to grow, though perhaps under appropriate discipline such as exclusion from the sacraments, were the impenitent sinners, the hypocrites, and the indifferent, but *not* the actively heretical and schismatic. These should be rooted out for the protection of the field.

In all that follows, this Protestant distinction between the visible and the invisible Church should be kept in mind. Always there was in the background the thought of the true, universal, spiritual Church. It was in the administration of the actual, visible, territorial churches and in the effort to keep these severally united in doctrine and structure that the Reformers took over and perpetuated the medieval pattern of procedure in their respective governmental areas.

Before detailing some of the ways in which the principal Protestant movements narrowed and hardened themselves into separate monolithic national churches, we must give full and emphatic recognition to the place that the total Church continued to have in the basic thought of the Reformers even while it was ceasing to manifest itself in their specific policies. This larger and more spiritual view of the Church finds expression in all the Reformation confessions and in the writings of all the great Reformers. The place it occupied in their thinking, and also the tension between it and the actual developments, are clearly expressed by J. T. McNeill in his chapter in *A History of the Ecumenical Movement:*

Not only through their appropriation of the ancient ecumenical Creeds, but also in the assertion of universal collective authority under Christ's Headship, the Reformers affirmed an ecumenical Church. The One Holy Catholic Church consists of all the faithful in all the world and through all time, and is ruled without a human monarch through representative assemblies under the

Word of God. Their doctrine always stressed the concept of the invisible or spiritual Church, but related with this is a more or less visible Church which is also Catholic. The conception of church reform was largely that of bringing the qualities of the invisible Church to visible expression.

The one true Catholic or universal Church, as they understood it, was not in their time to attain to convincing visibility. The leaders themselves came to sharp disagreement, especially on the doctrine of the Eucharist. Even where theology offered no barrier, national and linguistic boundaries limited fellowship. The conciliar or synodical organization of Lutheranism was seriously impaired through the control exercised by the territorial governments. The Reformed churches from the first adopted conciliar polities. Although they enjoyed much reciprocity, as organizations they were autonomous and never achieved international integration. Yet through the dark age of its progressive fissiparation Protestantism continued to crave an existential ecumenicity.[1]

One may perhaps be grateful that the national churches as they were in the sixteenth and seventeenth centuries did not "achieve international integration," since the method each of them adopted for achieving and maintaining its own unity and scope was such a close approximation to the medieval system against the Roman expression of which they were all in revolt.

Luther's initial statement about the character of the Church and the nature of its unity grew directly out of his epochal discovery of the principle of "justification by faith." In his tractate *The Babylonian Captivity of the Church* (1520), after speaking of the importance of baptism, he adds that "even so it is not baptism that justifies or benefits anyone, but it is faith in the word of promise, to which baptism is added." This faith must be personal and individual. In the same work, where he is showing that the benefits of the mass cannot be applied

[1] From *A History of the Ecumenical Movement, 1517-1948*, edited by Ruth Rouse and Stephen Charles Neill, 1954, The Westminster Press. Used by permission of The Westminster Press and S.P.C.K.

to anyone "save him alone who believes with a faith of his own," he continues:

Who can receive or apply in behalf of another, the promise of God, which demands the personal faith of every individual? Can I give to another what God has promised, even if he does not believe? Can I believe for another, or cause another to believe? But this is what I must do if I am able to apply and communicate the mass to others; for there are but two things in the mass— the promise of God and the faith of man which takes that which the promise offers. But if it is true that I can do this, then I can also hear and believe the gospel for others, I can be baptized for another, I can be absolved from sins for another, I can also partake of the sacrament of the altar for another, and—to run the gamut of their sacraments also—I can marry a wife for another, be ordained for another, receive confirmation and extreme unction for another! In fine, why did not Abraham believe for all the Jews? Why was faith in the promise made to Abraham demanded of every individual Jew? Therefore let this irrefutable truth stand fast. Where there is a divine promise everyone must stand upon his own feet, everyone's personal faith is demanded, everyone will give an account for himself and will bear his own burden.

It would be difficult to find anywhere a more unqualified assertion of the individual's personal responsibility for accepting or refusing the means of grace and for believing or not believing the gospel.

It is a natural inference that the true Church would consist of those, and only of those, who were believers, personally, individually, and voluntarily. This inference was immediately drawn, explicitly stated, and never repudiated. In his *Concerning Secular Authority* (1523) Luther asserts that "Christ desires to have a voluntary band of followers uncoerced, neither driven by law nor by the sword." In his *German Mass and Order of Worship* (1526) he repeats in substance the same description of the Church as consisting of those who had voluntarily accepted the gospel by faith. By the time the

126

Augsburg Confession was written (1530), the Lutheran churches were far from exemplifying that ideal, for they had already
become territorial or total-population churches. Nevertheless
the Church is still defined (Art. VII) as the "congregation of
saints (the assembly of all believers), in which the Gospel is
purely preached and the Sacraments rightly administered."

This, however, was not as decisive as it sounds, for in the
very next article (Art. VIII) the confession continues:

> Though the Church be properly the congregation of saints and
> true believers, yet seeing that in this life many hypocrites and evil
> persons are mingled with it, it is lawful to use the Sacraments
> administered by evil men, . . . And the Sacraments and the Word
> are effectual, by reason of the institution and commandment of
> Christ, though they be delivered by evil men. They condemn the
> Donatists and such like, who denied that it was lawful to use the
> ministry of evil men in the Church, and held that the ministry of
> evil men is useless and without effect.

The only part of this quotation that is significant for our
purpose is its first clause, in which there is an admission that
the Church may be actually something which it is not "properly." From that point the article diverges to discuss a quite
different point—not whether the Church should consist solely
of professed believers, but whether the validity of a sacrament
depends upon the moral virtue of the ministrant. On the
latter point the confession agrees with what has consistently
been the Catholic position and cites the heretical Donatists
to lend odium to the opposing position. But this issue is irrelevant for our present purpose, as it was to the really significant question in Luther's day.

The real questions which were posed by the definition of the
Church as the "congregation of saints" were these: (1) Should
infants be baptized and be recognized as members of the
Church, seeing that they cannot have that personal faith which
Luther had earlier insisted upon as absolutely essential to

justification and the establishment of a saving relationship with God? (2) Should persons be regarded as members of the Church simply because, being residents of the territory in which a church is dominant and being without any true faith of their own, they yield to social and political pressure and conform to its requirements rather than suffer exile or other civil punishment?

The first of these, the question of infant baptism, is interesting but must not divert us from giving our principal attention to the other. Luther got around it by assuming that a "latent faith" may exist even in newborn infants. Later defenders of infant baptism have found more plausible reasons for it. Luther's phrase sounds today less like a reason for his decision in favor of it than a somewhat strained explanation of a course that was determined on other grounds. One potent reason may have been that rejection of infant baptism was a mark of the hated and feared Anabaptists, with whom no responsible Christian leader could associate himself on a single point without losing prestige; another, carrying over the medieval Roman Catholic doctrine, that baptism *ex opere operato* was considered so essential to salvation that the Anabaptists could be condemned (Augsburg Confession, Art. IX) for affirming that children could be saved without it; a third, that the baptism of infants and their inclusion in the Church without actual faith was consistent with the total-population theory of church membership—the *Landeskirche*—which was quite evidently the pattern on which the Lutheran churches were going to develop. But our interest for the purposes of this discussion is not in the question of the baptism of infants but in the development of the territorial church and the means employed to give it the status and the monopoly which its nature demanded.

The second question, as has been stated, was whether the Church should actually be composed of believers or should include at least all the adult population of the governmental area. From this crucial question Luther shied away in his formal statements (as did Art. VIII of the Augsburg Confession) by diverting attention to two other questions, namely, (1) the validity of sacraments administered by "evil men" and (2) the question as to whether wicked or indifferent persons—who might very well be "believers" in the sense of formal compliance with the Church's doctrines and ritual requirements though not with its ethical standards—should be included in the membership of the Church. Neither of these touched the main issue. All but the utterly fanatical agreed that it would be intolerable to make the validity of sacraments dependent upon the virtue of the ministrant—a condition which in many cases could be known only to God. It could also be convincingly argued that, since the church at Corinth included the disorderly members whom Paul criticized so vigorously, it was never intended that the Church should be composed solely of the perfect. It was rather a school of virtue and of faith for the imperfect. But this admirable regard for human frailty and this rightful recognition of the Church's responsibility for a ministry to sinful men even within its own ranks did not dispose of the question as to whether enrollment in that school should be compulsory and virtually automatic for all who were resident within the governmental area of its jurisdiction. Without argument Luther decided that it should.

As soon as he became responsible for the pattern of church life in Saxony—not officially but by reason of his deserved influence and leadership—it became evident that he was committed to the plan of *Volkskirche,* or territorial Church, as against that of a Church of voluntary believers only. One can scarcely say that he made a deliberate decision to that effect, for it does not appear that it was ever an open question in his mind. He could think freely and profoundly about the nature of the Church universal as the body of Christ, and could show how it was to be distinguished from the apparatus of ecclesiastical government centering in Rome, so that revolt against the latter was not defection from the former. But when it came to deciding how the objective and visible Church was to be constituted in any specific area of government, the matter practically decided itself. As he saw it, there was only one possible course and no alternative. It would of course be a territorial Church including the whole population. Heretics must recant or take the consequences; dissenters must move out; no one could be allowed to stand on the sidelines neutral and uncommitted. No other kind of Church than that had been in existence since the days of Theodosius, barring some medieval heretical sects which had been snuffed out and perhaps some underground movements which all respectable persons regarded as fanatical and subversive. For Luther to have favored the voluntary Church would have been regarded as joining the Anabaptists, the only group in his time that believed in such a Church, and it was of course unthinkable that he should incur even a suspicion of sympathy with them in any matter. Moreover, Luther was interested in reforming the existing Church, making as few changes as possible and only those which fidelity to the gospel clearly required. Since the church in Saxony and the churches in the other German principalities where the evangelical cause won favor were already organized on the total-population pattern, the natural thing was to leave them so.

A modern Lutheran historian, Karl Holl, thus explains this determination in favor of the *Volkskirche:*

The area within which the local Church developed was everywhere determined by the boundaries of the political community. The reformatory movement which developed within a city had the natural tendency to sweep along the entire community. The goal was to make the civic community coincide with the Church community or fellowship. Luther himself considered this tie-up with the political form to be the demand of the hour.[2]

It was an equally inevitable "demand of the hour" that the idea of religious liberty within any given political jurisdiction should vanish from the picture, even while Luther continued

[2] Quoted in W. A. Mueller, *Church and State in Luther and Calvin* (Nashville: Broadman Press, 1954), p. 14.

to the end to insist upon the absolute necessity and the sole sufficiency of personal faith for man's justification with God. Luther's abandonment of religious liberty did not come immediately. In his *Concerning Secular Authority* (1523) he was saying that the state cannot use force against heretics. Three years later, comparing evangelicals with Roman Catholics, he wrote: "We do not kill, banish and persecute anyone who teaches other than we do. For we fight with the Word of God alone. If they do not want our witness, we let them have their way and separate ourselves from them and let them stick to any belief they like." A year later (1527) he favored banishing "false prophets." Karl Holl defends the thesis that Luther protected freedom of conscience by saying that no Roman Catholic was ever "persecuted" in Germany for his faith because a Roman Catholic could always migrate from a Lutheran to a Roman Catholic state! In 1530—the year of the Augsburg Confession—Luther approved the death penalty for Anabaptists which had been decreed by that same Diet of Speyer (1529) at which the protest of the Evangelicals against its inequitable treatment of themselves in comparison with the Roman Catholics earned them the name of "Protestants." He supported this position by quoting Moses on the stoning of blasphemers. In 1531 the normally mild-mannered and conciliatory Melanchthon urged the death penalty for those who spoke against the rightfulness of the clerical office, on the ground that this was "sedition," and in 1536 he instigated the execution of several Anabaptists at Jena. While the Anabaptists were the most warmly hated and the most rigorously punished of all the non-Lutherans, a similar attitude was expressed, though not with actual fire and sword, toward Zwinglians, Jews, and (a little later) Calvinists.

The part which the civil government was to play in Luther's theory and practice of reformation was forecast in his *Address to the Christian Nobles of the German Nation* (1520). His appeal to the nobles was on the ground that the responsibility for reforming the Church rested upon the laity since the Church essentially *was* its laity, who constituted its universal priest-hood, and that it rested primarily on the nobles and princes because they were the laymen who were in a position to take effective action. As one after another of them did take effective action in supporting the reform, the theory developed into a fuller recognition of the special status of rulers as guardians of the faith. The Augsburg Confession was addressed to Emperor Charles V. It was signed not by the theologians and learned clergy but by seven rulers, including the dukes of Saxony and Lüneburg, the margrave of Brandenburg, the landgrave of Hesse, and the prince of Anhalt, and by the senate and magis-tracy of Nuremberg and the senate of Reutlingen. Every German ruler of a Protestant state became a little Constantine to confirm, if not to determine, the lines of orthodox doctrine and a little Theodosius to enforce its acceptance upon all his sub-jects.

Cuius regio eius religio—"He who rules the territory con-trols its religion"—became the accepted formula for determin-ing the religious coloration of each state within the Empire and the religious rights of the subjects of each prince. This prin-ciple was foreshadowed in the concessions by the Diet of Speyer (1526) which gave the evangelicals their first legal toe hold. It was made explicit in the Peace of Augsburg (1555) and was confirmed and extended by the Peace of Westphalia (1648) at the end of the Thirty Years' War. This was the guar-antee of unity for each territorial church.

The purpose of this survey is not to present a complete ac-count of Luther's doctrine of the Church, which had many ad-mirable and fruitful features, but to focus attention upon his concept of the conditions of unity in a territorial Church and the way in which it was to be maintained. The Church was united if, and only if, it included all the Christians within a given jurisdiction in which all citizens were required to be Christians, and if all these Christians accepted the authorized doctrinal formulas and consented to the established forms of polity and worship, so that neither heresy nor schism would exist within the area. The methods of attaining this happy condition included (1) the careful catechetical training of the young and (2) the application of force by imprisonment, banishment, or execution to suppress or eliminate persistent dissenters. The first of these must never be overlooked or underestimated as perpetuating the core of faith and devotion within the Church. The second was essential to the unity of the Church if it was to have an authoritative standard of doctrine and polity accepted, either actively or passively, by the entire population of the state.

Lutheranism entered the Scandinavian countries early and successfully. As in England almost simultaneously, and in Scotland only a little later, political events reinforced a religious awakening to produce the complete dominance of the Protestant cause. Under the patriot leader who freed Sweden from the overlordship of Denmark and became King Gustavus Vasa, the independence of Sweden from Copenhagen and from Rome became the two aspects of a single campaign of liberation. The entire structure of the church in Sweden was taken over, bishops and all, and with it inevitably the concept of the *Volkskirche* and of an all-inclusive national church—based, as it turned out, on the Augsburg Confession and the Lutheran cultus—as not only itself a unified body but a unifying factor in the national life. That this view of the Church and its unity is still firmly held and strongly defended in Sweden is made evident by a scholarly volume published in English under the title *This Is the Church,* edited by Bishop Nygren, which is a translation of the greater part of an outstanding work issued in Swedish in 1945. This symposium by some of the ablest minds in the Church of Sweden defends the position that a state church having a membership practically coextensive with the entire population of the country, regardless of personal faith, repentance, or commitment, is an arrangement good for the church, good for the country, and perfectly in harmony with the New Testament concept of the Church and with a sound theology of the Church.

The case of the Church of Sweden is cited here because it illustrates with exceptional clarity the process by which in the Protestant state churches interest in the unity of the whole Church was superseded by a more urgent concern for the unity of the national organization and the inclusion of the entire population within it. The Augsburg Confession's admirable definition of the "true Church" became a part of Sweden's official faith when that confession was adopted as the doctrinal standard, and doubtless it was sincerely believed by those who gave the matter any thought. The true and universal Church, of which only God could know the exact boundaries, was necessarily and inherently one; but recognition of this truth could have little effect on the actual policies and attitudes of the functioning organization. The practical problem was not so much to unite the Church as to unite the people of Sweden in one Swedish national church. Action by the state was the chief agency in producing that result. A minimum of pressure was sufficient for this because no actual conformity to the doctrines or practices of the church was required in order to qualify one for retaining membership in it. Full liberty was given to dissenting bodies, but until 1952 it was legally impossible for anyone who had been baptized in the Church of Sweden (as nearly everyone was) to get out of it except by joining some other church. In that year the membership was given as 87 per cent of the population but was reported as the "church community" rather than as members.[3]

The teaching of Calvin and the practice of the Reformed churches tended to stress the view of the Church as a juridically organized and competently functioning body—that is, the regional Church visible. Whether this was more true of Calvin

---

[3] A former Methodist superintendent in Sweden told me that half the Methodists in that country remained technically members of the Church of Sweden.

than of Luther is a moot question which does not require an answer here. Calvin, like Luther, did not forget the Church universal, but the duty that pressed upon him was the reformation of religion in Geneva and in the other governmental areas in which his influence prevailed or might prevail. That influence became widely international, and even more so after his death, extending throughout Switzerland and to France, Germany, the Netherlands, Scotland, England, and the American colonies.

Calvin clearly distinguished between two kinds of "Church," both of which he regarded as essential:

I have observed that the Scriptures speak of the Church in two ways. . . . [1] the Church as it really is before God—the Church into which none are admitted but those who by the gift of adoption are sons of God, and by the sanctification of the Spirit true members of Christ . . . [and, 2] the whole body of mankind who profess to worship one God and Christ, who by baptism are initiated into the faith. . . . In this Church there is a very large mixture of hypocrites, who have nothing of Christ but the outward name and appearance; of ambitious, avaricious, envious, evil-speaking men, some also of impure lives, who are tolerated for a time, either because their guilt cannot be legally established, or because due strictness of discipline is not always observed.[4]

God's eternal and immutable decrees determining how many and who were to be saved and his calling of the elect were regarded as positive and known theological truths, but the impact of the divine action on specific individuals was shrouded in mystery. No one could know with certainty who were called. Thus no clear line could be drawn between the true Church of the redeemed and the "mighty company of the damned." It was therefore the part of charity to hold within the visible Church all who did not virtually cut themselves off by obvious heresy or schism, and it was the part of piety and wisdom to

[4] *Institutes* II. iv. 19-20.

discipline known offenders so far as might be and to invoke the aid of the magistrates to protect the community against contamination of morals or corruption of doctrine. It would, of course, be the responsibility of the Church, acting through its properly constituted agencies, to establish the standards of conduct and doctrine which the magistrates were to enforce. As with Luther so with Calvin and with multitudes of the followers of both from that day to this, the charitable and even necessary inclusion of hypocritical and sinful professed believers in the actual church of a community along with the sincere and relatively virtuous believers became the excuse (if one were needed) for including the entire body of citizens regardless of their wish to be included. As a matter of fact, the total-population theory of the Church was so firmly established by centuries of precedent that, so far as I have been able to discover from his writings, Calvin never seriously considered the possibility of any alternative.

In view of the function assigned to the civil government as the protecter of faith and morals, the theory of the state became important. Archbishop Cyril Garbett, writing of church and state in England, has rightly said: "There is no complete theory of the state in the New Testament; the first Christians had no need to define their attitude towards it, for they were convinced that the world and all its glory would soon pass away." The New Testament did offer three good texts: "The powers that be are ordained of God." (Rom. 13:1.) "Put them in mind to be subject to principalities and powers, to obey magistrates." (Tit. 3:1.) "Fear God. Honour the king." (I Pet. 2:17.) And if apostles could enjoin such subjection to pagan rulers, how much more, it could be argued, should homage and obedience be rendered to Christian kings and governments. The Geneva Confession of 1536 (Article 21) declared:

We hold the supremacy and dominion of kings and princes as also of other magistrates and officers, to be a holy thing and a good ordinance of God. . . . In sum, we ought to regard them as vicars and lieutenants of God, whom we cannot resist without resisting God himself.

If this strong language leads anyone to suspect that Calvinists were committed to the theory of the divine right of kings and to a policy of nonresistance under all circumstances, the whole history of Presbyterianism in Scotland and Puritanism in England and of both in colonial America furnishes a complete refutation of that idea. James I, the most eminent exponent of the divine right of kings in his times, got no comfort from his Presbyterian subjects in his native Scotland or from the Puritans in England, and they got none from him; and the Puritans were so far from regarding Charles I as the "vicar of God" not to be resisted "without resisting God himself" that they beheaded him. Resistance to royal power could scarcely go further!

Nevertheless Calvin and his European followers held fast to the thought that it was the business of the government to support and defend the true faith and to protect the church within its jurisdiction from the competition of variant doctrines and the infiltration of false doctrines as well as to protect the community from moral laxity. The Gallican Confession of 1559, of which Calvin was the principal author, guarded against subordination of the church to the state by saying (Art. 26): "We believe . . . that all jointly should keep and maintain the union of the Church, and submit to the public teaching and to the yoke of Jesus Christ wherever God shall have established a true order of the Church, even if the magistrates and their edicts are contrary to it." That this was not said in the spirit of defiance is shown by the statement (Art. 39) that "God has put the sword into the hand of magistrates to suppress crimes against the first as well as against the second table of the Commandments of God," and that Christians must hold magistrates in all reverence as God's "lieutenants and officers, whom he has commissioned to exercise a legitimate and holy authority."

Perhaps the whole matter can be best summed up in Calvin's own words concerning the functions of civil government, which are:

to foster and maintain the external worship of God, to defend sound doctrine and the condition of the Church, to adapt our conduct to human society, to form our manners to civil justice, to conciliate us to each other, to cherish common peace and tranquility.[5]

The objective of the entire religio-political regime in Geneva under Calvin's predominating influence was to create and maintain what later came to be called a "holy state," that is to say, a community which would be a political state in one aspect and a church in another. Church and state would have identical membership, and the community would be kept free from doctrinal deviation and moral laxity by the combined forces of teaching and discipline by the church and wise legislation and civil punishments by the state. The continuous and long-sustained pressure for the maintenance of Calvinistic orthodoxy and the enforcement of a rigid code of conduct worked surprisingly well for a good many years. It is remarkable, in view of the customs of the time and the history of similar policies of enforced conformity elsewhere, that such a thorough suppression of religious liberty was attained with so little violence. The one episode which attracted most attention and has been the occasion for the most criticism was the burning of Servetus. Considering the burnings and hangings for heresy that had been going on by the hundreds all over Europe for centuries and that were still going on in the sixteenth century in both Catholic and Protestant lands, the emphasis that historians have given to this isolated instance in Calvin's Geneva is most unfair, and it may seem ungenerous

[5] *Ibid.*, II. iv. 521.

to cite it now. Nevertheless it would be an evasion to omit it, for it was logically consistent with the type of regime under which it occurred.

Servetus, one among several liberal-minded Spaniards of his time, was a somewhat unstable and temperamental genius with remarkable gifts as a scientist and with a scientist's predilection for freedom of thought in theology. He discovered the circulation of the blood in the lungs long before Harvey made his more complete discovery. His theology does not seem fatally heretical to most people today who take the trouble to learn what it was, but it was certainly not Calvinism. It had already got him into trouble with the Spanish inquisition and he had been imprisoned but escaped. Servetus and Calvin had engaged in some controversial correspondence which had become rather sharply personal, and Servetus had been warned to stay away from Geneva. But courage or bravado prevailed over caution, and he came. He was arrested, tried for heresy, condemned, and burned. It was not Calvin who passed the sentence, but he consented to it and must bear the heavy moral responsibility for the event.

Modern Roman Catholics, who are as averse to such procedures as Protestants, often mention the burning of Servetus as parallel and equivalent to the proceedings of the Inquisition. In extenuation of Calvin's inexcusable act some differences may be mentioned. The burning of Servetus was a single act which sent such a wave of horror through the Protestant communities that it was never repeated. It did not have the approval of the whole Church or any part of it much longer than it took the fire to burn down. It may be noted that the year of the Servetus tragedy (1553) was the very year in which Mary Tudor began her reign in England. Her systematic burning of Protestants brought nearly sixty to the stake for each of the five years of her reign. Quantitatively the burning of one man under Calvin's rule does not balance the burning of two thousand under the inquisitorship of Torquemada and many more thousands before his time. The trial was conducted without torture and without forced or secret testimony, unlike the practice of the Inquisition. Personal enmity may have been a factor, but greed was not, for the persecutors were not enriched, as in Spain, by the confiscation of the victim's property. The act has been disavowed in penitence and sackcloth by Calvin's church. Many years ago the Genevan and French Protestants erected an "expiatory monument" on the site of the burning, and the street leading to it has been named "Rue de Michel Servet." In short, the burning of Servetus was an episode, not a crusade.

It was, however, a significant episode because it revealed the danger inherent in the system which produced it. When Church and state make alliance to utilize the power of the state for the maintenance of a certain body of religious doctrine and practice in the entire community, and to utilize this religious homogeneity for the community's political unification, the use of compulsory and punitive measures becomes inevitable. When the great state churches of classical Protestantism accepted that heritage from the medieval Church, they received its liabilities as well as its assets. The assets were: security in areas where the governments could be brought to their side; the prestige of being *the* church within the areas of their respective dominance; the immediate adherence of large numbers of people who were accustomed to going along with the prevailing regime; the exercise of moral control, which might be beneficent though harsh, over the entire community. The liabilities were: the sacrifice of the religious liberty which had been presupposed as essential in the beginning of their movements; confusion and contradiction between their definition of the Church as being composed of sincere (and that means voluntary) believers and their policy of total-population membership and compulsory conformity; entanglement in political situations in a period of turbulent political life.

When the European leaders of the Reformation thought of a

united Church in the widest sense—as they often did, for the ecumenical ideal was an element in their hopes—they thought of such an agreement among the territorial churches on a common formulation of doctrine and such mutual recognition of one another's ministries and polities as would permit free co-operation and interchange among organizations which would still preserve their identity and character as the churches of their respective nations. This was also the intent of the work of John Dury, that ardent apostle of irenics who shuttled from one European court to another through a good part of the seventeenth century, busily promoting peace and concord among the national churches.

The burning of Servetus, by arousing widespread protest, "lighted a candle" of liberty which was not to be put out. Many factors operated in ending the regime of intolerance and compulsory church unity in Protestant countries. One of them was a book by Sebastian Castellio, *Concerning Heretics,* published in 1554, the year after the burning of Servetus. It was a carefully argued denunciation of that crime against liberty and all the presuppositions on which it was based. Castellio, an able scholar, had earlier been brought to Geneva by Calvin to serve as rector of the college, but theological disagreements had caused him to move to Basel. Theodore Beza, Calvin's associate and lieutenant, published a reply defending the burning, the system which had led to it, and the whole Calvinistic program. Castellio's book was widely read throughout Europe. In the Netherlands it was translated into Dutch and popularized by the Erasmian scholar Coornhert. James Arminius, who had studied under Beza, was selected to write an answer but was converted by studying the book he had been commissioned to refute and came out against both the persecution of dissenters and the Calvinistic doctrine of predestination.

The case of the Netherlands was different from that of the other European countries. While strong Protestant churches

were being established in the German and Scandinavian states
and in Switzerland, the Low Countries were for several decades
the victim of a Spanish crusade to crush at once the rising spirit
of political independence and the growing Protestant movement. Thus patriotism and Protestantism became correlative
terms. William of Orange, at that time a Catholic, in petition-
ing Philip II to revoke his cruel anti-Protestant edicts, wrote:
"I am a Catholic and will not deviate from my religion, but I
cannot approve the custom of kings to confine men's creeds
and religion within arbitrary limits." But he did deviate, and
after he became Protestant, he urged (1572) his associates and
subordinates "to restore fugitives and those banished for conscience' sake, and to see that the Word of God is preached,
without however suffering any hindrance to the Roman Catholic Church in the practice of its religion." The five northern
provinces, joined in the Union of Utrecht, declared their independence of Spain (1581) and soon made good that declaration. The Fundamental Laws of the new nation affirmed (Art.
13) the principle of religious toleration, even while the church,
which had meanwhile accepted the Presbyterian polity and the
Calvinistic system of theology, became the state church. Controversy over the Arminian deviation from Calvinism, coming
to a crisis at the Synod of Dort (1618-19), complicated by a
simultaneous struggle for power between the central government and the states, led to a brief period of religious intolerance. It was in that period that the Dutch founded New
Amsterdam, which was later to become New York, but the few
years of Dutch intolerance had already passed by the time
Governor Peter Stuyvesant tried to make the colony a closed
preserve for the Dutch Reformed Church—less from religious
zeal than from his temperamental addiction to arbitrary rule—
so that the home government had to intervene and reverse
his policy. The Netherlands had its established church, but
more quickly than any other country in Europe it learned the
lesson of history, that compulsory religious homogeneity is

no road to domestic peace, national strength, or church unity in the modern world. So Holland became the place of refuge for men of other countries who were persecuted for conscience' sake. England was to learn the same lesson later and only after a longer and more bitter struggle.

Chapter VI

The Second Revolution

BREAKDOWN OF MEDIEVAL TYPE
OF UNITY

MUCH HAS BEEN SAID ABOUT "INTOLERANCE," AND MORE MAY
yet be said in the succeeding chapters. The topic is unavoidable when the unity of the Church is under consideration.
For clarification some comments should be made about the
use of this term and its opposite, "toleration."

In general, modern men of good will are accustomed to
regard it as meritorious to be tolerant and blameworthy to be
intolerant. On the other hand, there are those who say that
intolerance is only a righteous zeal for the truth and that the
sole reason for tolerance is indifference to the issues involved.
These opposing opinions both contain some degree of truth.
Tolerance is not always a virtue, nor intolerance always a vice.
Intolerance is often spurred by zeal for a good cause, and
indifference is sometimes, but not always, the motive for toleration. No evaluation of either attitude in a particular case can
be made without taking into account: (1) the nature of the
opinion or behavior which is to be either tolerated or not
tolerated; (2) the nature of the community or organization
within which these varieties of thought or conduct occur; (3)
the specific ways in which intolerance manifests itself; (4) the
natural human rights, and sometimes the legal rights, of the
persons involved; and (5) the long-run social effects of adopting one of these attitudes or the other.

144

Religious intolerance is of two kinds, civil and ecclesiastical. The first of these is the refusal to permit the propagation, or even the very existence, of a variant religious opinion within the state. In Christian countries this presupposes: that the state as well as the church will suffer irreparable damage if the variant view is held and taught; that there is a church with a fixed body of doctrine and an institutional structure which together constitute the standard by which all other forms of religious belief and behavior are to be measured; that such a relation exists between church and state that the police power of the state can be utilized to suppress deviations and thus protect the unity of the one legal church in that area and insure the allegiance of the entire population to it; that the proposed measures of coercion would not invade any human rights which either church or state is under any obligation to respect. The indispensable tool of civil intolerance in religion is persecution or some form of restraint and restriction which falls only a little short of it. A church which exercises the power of a state may commit this kind of intolerance.

The second, or ecclesiastical, form of religious intolerance is the refusal by a church to permit the existence of variant religious opinions or certain specific variants of belief or behavior within its own membership, regardless of what attitude the state may adopt. When the state does not lend its resources to provide civil penalties and the church does not have its own police power, the normal process is the exclusion of the dissenters or their voluntary withdrawal from fellowship with the group from whose position they dissent. The inevitable consequence of this is sectarianism. It is the responsibility of every church to determine for itself the degree of detail with which it will define its standards of doctrine and conduct and the degree of tolerance it will exercise toward those of its members who do not completely conform to these standards.

In Chapter III we considered the unity of the Church in a period (the second and third centuries and the first part of the fourth) in which only ecclesiastical intolerance was exercised. The term is used here without opprobrium. No judgment is being passed on the legitimacy of the process by which the Church maintained what we have called "unity by exclusion." Under the conditions of that time how could it have remained united in the maintenance of its increasingly precise definition of doctrine and in submission to its more and more closely integrated system of ecclesiastical authority except by declaring that those who did not conform to the first and submit to the second were no part of the Church?

In Chapters IV and V we discussed the very long period—actually more than half the total history of Christianity—during which ecclesiastical intolerance was reinforced by civil intolerance. During all these centuries, from the fourth to the seventeenth, dissent (labeled heresy or schism) was treated as both a sin against God and a crime against the state, and every effort was made to suppress it by both ecclesiastical and civil penalties, that is, by both excommunication and persecution. The procedure of the Inquisition represents this phase at its peak of perfection. The culprit was first examined (under torture), condemned and excommunicated by the Church, and was then "remitted to the secular arm" and burned. The great Protestant churches on the continent, as we have seen, carried out the same general policy, though with less efficient apparatus and seldom to such a fatal extreme. They had abandoned many features of the medieval church, but they held fast to the two basic ideas which determined the nature of its unity and the means of preserving it: first, that the unity of the Church required total agreement on a complete system of doctrine set forth in authorized creeds and confessions and allegiance to its centralized institutional structure; and second, that the religious homogeneity of the entire population on these terms was essential both to the stability of the state and to the honor of the Church. With the breaking up of the Empire and the rise of autonomous nations and principalities,

146

church unity as a practical problem had come to mean the unity of the church within a given governmental area.

Now we have to consider how the church in England illustrated this same pattern of thought and action, continuing for a time to maintain the medieval system of unity, subject only to the changes that grew out of the separateness of the nation as an independent political entity, and then how that medieval type of unity broke down with the rise of modern ideas of civil and religious liberty. Since this book is not a history of the Church but only a study of its changing concepts of unity and the means of attaining it, the story of the English Reformation need not be recited. It has been competently told by many historians. It will be sufficient for our purpose to note the principal facts that are directly relevant to our theme.

The contribution of Henry VIII to the English Reformation was virtually limited to the detachment of the church in England from its allegiance to Rome. The statement, often made by the ill-informed, that he "founded the Church of England" contains far more error than truth. The degree of truth it does contain rests upon an ambiguity in the term "church." In England, as in other lands that were becoming Protestant, the word had three distinguishable meanings: first, the Church invisible; second, the whole visible Church considered as an institution having a continuous existence from its beginning and extending throughout Christendom; third, the church as an organized structure within the nation. Some, but not all, believed that the continuity of the Church (in the second sense) and thus its present reality depended upon the continuity of its episcopate. Others, while recognizing that the Church had had an unbroken history as a visible institution and a body of believers, held that the Church existed in full validity "wherever the gospel is truly preached and the sacraments are rightly administered." The first of these two views prevailed in England. All Protestants agreed that the true churchly character of a church (in the third sense) did not depend upon subordination to or connection with the ecclesiastical structure centering in Rome. Henry VIII had his own political and personal reasons for agreeing with the continental Protestants on this latter point while he disapproved almost all their other proposals for reform. Before the separation issue came up, the pope had bestowed on Henry the title "Defender of the Faith," for a treatise the king had written in rebuttal of Luther. Whatever his motives for separating, it was in his reign and on his initiative that the Church (second sense) *in* England became the Church (third sense) *of* England. In his view and in the view of all intelligent Anglicans thereafter the valid churchliness of the Church of England depends upon the fact that he did not "found" it but simply detached it from a usurping authority which had never been essential to its validity and had now become hostile to its best interests.

With the separation from Rome and the accompanying stress on what I have called "church in the third sense," or the national church, the question of unity of the church became as a practical administrative matter that of maintaining the unity of this national church. It was a real problem because of the diversity of religious views in sixteenth-century England, and it grew more difficult as the century advanced. There were Catholics who resented and resisted the separation from Rome. There were other Catholics who, like King Henry, wanted no change other than that. There were the Lollards, the inheritors of the Wycliffe tradition, a kind of evangelical underground of problematical but by no means negligible proportions. There were the humanists at the universities and among the clergy, men who as students of Greek had directed their attention to the New Testament and as Renaissance men of Erasmian temper were restless under any ecclesiastical authority which restricted their freedom of thought and research. There were those who had read with approval Luther's writings—his Nintey-five Theses and his three Reformation tractates of 1520 —and the Lutheran literature in the years immediately following. (The Augsburg Confession of 1530 was already in print and widely circulated before Henry's break with Rome.) The influence of Calvin had begun to be felt in England before the end of Henry's reign; it became stronger under Edward VI; Mary's attempt to re-establish Catholicism drove to Geneva many who escaped the flames of her persecutions, and these came back under Elizabeth more strongly Protestant and more Calvinistic than they had been before. This Genevan influence was the principal source of English Puritanism. In addition there was the Anabaptist strain which, cleansing itself of the fanatical and anarchistic features which had marred some of its communities on the continent, entered England as a small and inconspicuous company but carrying a germinal idea that was destined to have a mighty growth, for the Anabaptists— who became Baptists in England—were at that time the only consistent exponents of the concept of the Church as a fellowship of believers all of whom had become members of the Church by their own voluntary act.

How could there be a united national church including the entire population of England when there were such varieties of belief and practice? The difficulty was occasioned by the attempt to satisfy two conditions: first, that the church must include the whole population in its membership; second, that it must hold its members to the acceptance of a uniform standard of doctrine and a uniform pattern of worship and polity. Both were, as we have seen, essential features of the medieval concept of unity. Both seemed so axiomatic in the period of the Reformation that it was only infrequently that anyone took the trouble to reaffirm them. Richard Hooker makes the first of these principles clear enough in his famous work *The Laws of Ecclesiastical Polity* (1594) : "There is not any man of the Church of England but the same man is not also a member of the Commonwealth, nor any member of the Commonwealth which is not also of the Church of England." [1] A more recent formulation of the same idea, showing how the ideal has persisted even long after its realization has become

[1] Bk. VIII. 1-2.

apparently unattainable, is in these words written by Bishop Creighton in 1899: "Church and State are the nation looked at from different points of view. The nation looked at from the secular side is the State, looked at from the religious side it is the Church, and separation between the two is impossible." [2]

Every historian of the period finds it necessary to take into account the prevalence of this total-population theory of the church, without which the policies of both state and church at that time would be unintelligible. An Anglican historian, discussing the Elizabethan settlement, writes:

It was only natural that a settlement which had been arrived at by the deliberate adoption of a middle course between the extremes of Romanish medievalism on the one hand and advanced Protestantism on the other, should meet with determined opposition from both these quarters. It was also not to be expected that, in an age when the toleration of varying forms of religious belief was an idea that only existed in the imagination of a few philosophical visionaries, any deliberate want of conformity with the established religious system would be permitted with impunity. [3]

The Elizabethan settlement was indeed a triumph of political policy and able statesmanship which as such merits the admiration even of those who think that something better could be said of the toleration of varying religious beliefs, even then, than that it was a vagary of "philosophical visionaries." That a highly intelligent modern clerical scholar could describe it only in these terms shows what an aura of sanctity has come to envelop this medieval concept of essential churchliness as demanding compulsory state-wide conformity to an established religious order. One gets the impression that many of these commentators regard this as having been a grand system while

[2] Quoted in Hugh Martin, *Christian Reunion: A Plea for Action* (London: Macmillan Co., 1941), p. 164.

[3] C. Sydney Carter, *The English Church and the Reformation* (New York: Longmans, Green & Co., 1925), p. 224.

it lasted—though of course they deplore the persecution without which it never could have existed—and that they cannot think of its present impracticability without at least a tinge of regret. This may account for the fact that Troeltsch's famous designation of the totalitarian pattern as the "church-type church," relegating the voluntary church to an obviously inferior category as the "sect-type," has been so often and so enthusiastically quoted by representatives of national churches.

The late Archbishop of York confirms the description that has been given of the concept of church unity in England in the sixteenth and seventeenth centuries, and adds the important consideration that it was held by all, or almost all, parties:

There was one great assumption beneath the quarrels and negotiations between Church and State in the Middle Ages and in the century immediately after the Reformation. It was taken for granted that the citizens of the same nation all belonged to the same Church; if there were obstinate dissidents, for the sake of the State and the good of their souls they must either be converted or liquidated. . . . In England until the seventeenth century it was assumed that there would be only one Church for the nation. Anglicans, Presbyterians, and Puritans attempted to fashion the Church into their special pattern. . . . Most of [the established churches] are survivals of the day when there was only one Church in the nation.[4]

The Elizabethan settlement determined what were to be the main characteristics of the Church of England. It was to be episcopal in structure.[5] It was to be liturgical in worship, using

[4] Garbett, *op. cit.*, pp. 21, 23. Used by permission of Hodder & Stoughton Ltd.

[5] The acceptance of episcopacy in the Church of England, or rather its continuance after the separation from Rome, did not at first necessarily imply the belief that an authentic church or a valid ministry could not exist without it. Bishop John Hooper of Gloucester (1551): "The Church is bound to no sort of ministers or any ordinary succession of bishops, but only unto the Word of God." Bishop Cooper of Winchester recognized the legitimacy of the continental Protestant churches without bishops and said the reason the English did not follow their pattern was that they did not think it fitted the "state

151

a revision of the Edward VI *Book of Common Prayer* in the English language. The Thirty-nine Articles were to be its doctrinal standard. Its ministers were to wear clerical vestments, and certain ceremonial acts resembling those of Roman Catholicism were to be continued. The royal supremacy over church as well as state was to be acknowledged. The theory of religious homogeneity as essential to national strength and security was as it always had been—everyone must conform to the requirements of one national church. But Elizabeth, though an obstinate woman, was a wise queen. In practice she did not press the demand for conformity beyond the limit of the attainable. The laity were for the most part left undisturbed. It was known that Roman Catholic priests could not take the oath recognizing the queen as supreme head of the church, so most of them were allowed to evade the issue. Elizabeth did burn some Roman Catholics—almost as many in the forty-five years of her reign as the Protestants whom Mary burned in her five years—but only those who were believed to be engaged in active conspiracy to assassinate or dethrone her after the pope had excommunicated her and released all her subjects from their allegiance. There were Puritan ministers in the church, many of whom avoided conformity and escaped discipline for years. When some of them withdrew from the churches and began to assemble the people to hear "lectures," thus forming what were in effect dissenting congregations and building up a great body of convinced Puritan laity, no effective preventive measures were taken until a new and more rigorous Archbishop of Canterbury came in late in her reign.

It was not that the Puritans were in principle any more tolerant of diversity within the church or within the nation than were the advocates of episcopacy. That became evident

---

of our country, people or commonwealth." J. D. Hunkin, later bishop of Truro, in his *The Call for Christian Unity* summarized the evidence that the idea of apostolic succession as necessary came late to the Church of England. Bishop Henson in *The Church of England* speaks of the "sinister and unprecedented" emphasis on episcopacy after the Savoy Conference of 1661. These citations are from *Christian Reunion* by Hugh Martin.

when the harsh policy of the Stuart kings and of Archbishop
Laud had forced the great Puritan migration to America,
where they set up a regime to their liking and attempted to
build a "holy state" on the Geneva pattern. Few of them
were by choice separatists from the Church of England. Their
desire was primarily to make it a Puritan church. The alliance of episcopacy with the royal absolutism of James I and
Charles I tended to produce an opposing alliance of Puritanism
with the cause of Parliamentary government, and thus ultimately put it on the side of the growing demand for civil and
religious liberty. Calvinism, even in its most rugged days in
Geneva, had always tended toward equalitarianism and the
challenging of the absoluteness of any human authority.

During the period of Puritan dominance in England the left-
wing minority groups and the independents and free spirits
within the complex totality of Puritanism furnished some elo-
quent and courageous champions of freedom. One of the
earliest and most famous was John Milton, whose *Areopagitica*
was a Puritan's protest to a Puritan Parliament against its tyran-
nical suppression of "unlicensed printing." For three hundred
years it has been a fundamental document in any campaign
for freedom of the press, but underlying its concern for that
particular freedom was a comprehensive demand for civil and
religious liberty of a sort and on a scale that England had
never known.

In the year after the execution of Charles I, when the Presbyterian Puritans seemed to be firmly in power, another left-
wing Puritan expressed sentiments in accord with Milton's:

Let there be liberty of the press for printing, to those that are not
allowed pulpits for preaching. Let that light come in at the win-
dow which cannot come in at the door, that all may speak and
write one way that cannot another. . . . Let there be free debate
and open conference and communication, for all and of all sorts
that will, concerning difference in spirituals; still allowing the
state to secure all tumults or disturbances. Where doors are not

shut, there will be no breaking them open. So where debates are free there is a way of vent and evacuation, the stopping of which hath caused more troubles in states than anything; for where there is much new wine in old bottles the working will be such as the parable speaks on.[6]

The Puritan separatists, or Independents, found a spokesman in Henry Overton, whose argument for religious liberty was published (1645) under the cautious title *The Ancient Bounds; or, Liberty of Conscience, Tenderly Stated, Modestly asserted, and mildly vindicated:*

In policy 'tis the worst way in the world and will prove the least successful, to extirpate errors by force. For this multiplies them rather, even as the Bishops' tyrannies did drive men to extremities, and we may thank their strict urging of conformity and uniformity as the instrumental cause and means of those extremities of absolute separation and Anabaptism, which many honest and tender hearts, thinking they could never run far enough from the Bishops, did run into. . . . And who knows but, if force were removed and a league made, and free trading of truth set on foot, and liberty given to try all things, straying brethren on the right hand might be reduced? . . . Now this trying and judging is in vain if there be not a liberty of profession; and to hinder this were a most tyrannous usurpation over the connection which God hath made between the understanding and the will, and to put asunder what God hath joined together, and indeed to violate the law of God and nature. A man cannot will contrary to the precedent act of judgment; he wills weakly without an act of judgment preceding. To force a man to a profession or practice which he wills not, nay, which he nills, is to offer unto God a sacrifice of violence on the part of the compulsor, and an unreasonable service on the part of the compelled, and therefore necessarily unacceptable.[7]

[6] John Saltmarsh, *Smoke in the Temple* (1646).

[7] For much other documentary material illustrating the Puritan assertion of the principle of religious liberty, with selections from John Lilburne, Robert Greville, John Goodwin, William Walwyn, Henry Robinson, and others, see the following:

Though Roger Williams is best known for his work in America, his experiment with liberty in Rhode Island and his clash with John Cotton, he got his training in England. In his best-known book he wrote:

An enforced uniformity of religion throughout a nation or civil state confounds the civil and the religious, denies the principles of Christianity and civility, and that Jesus Christ is come in the flesh. The permission of other consciences and worships than a state professeth only can, according to God, procure a firm and lasting peace; good assurance being taken, according to the wisdom of the civil state, for uniformity of civil obedience from all sorts. True civility and Christianity may both flourish in a state or kingdom, notwithstanding the permission of divers and contrary consciences, either of Jew or Gentile.[8]

As Milton had sounded his trumpet note on freedom of the press shortly after the beginning of the Puritan interval in England's history, so he returned to the battle for liberty on a wider field when a new era of enforced conformity with Anglican episcopacy was imminent with the return of Charles II. Some irenic spirits had been pleading for a "comprehensive" Church which could include all Christians by requiring of them only the "essentials" which were held by all and permitting variety in "nonessentials." To this the rigid authoritarians who wanted total conformity could reply that if certain things, such as ceremonies and episcopal polity, were rated by these unionists as nonessential, then the rejection of them must also be nonessential, so it was unreasonable to make an issue of them if authority imposed them. In reply to this, and on the whole subject of regulating religion by law, Milton wrote:

William Haller, ed., *Tracts on Liberty in the Puritan Revolution, 1638-1647* (New York: Columbia University Press, 1934), 3 vols.

W. K. Jordan, *The Development of Religious Toleration in England* (from the beginning of the Reformation to 1660) (Cambridge, Mass.: Harvard University Press, 1932-40), 4 vols.

A. S. P. Woodhouse, ed., *Puritanism and Liberty* (University of Chicago Press, 1951).

[8] *The Bloudy Tenent of Persecution for the Cause of Conscience* (1644).

I have shown that the civil power neither hath right nor can do right by forcing religious things. I will now show the wrong it doth by violating the fundamental privilege of the Gospel, the new birthright of every true believer, Christian liberty. . . . They who would seem more knowing confess that these things [certain ceremonies and orders] are indifferent, but for that very cause by the magistrate may be commanded. As if God of his special grace in the Gospel had to this end freed us from his own commandments in these things, that our freedom should subject us to a more grievous yoke, the commandments of men! As well may the magistrate call that common or unclean which God hath cleansed . . . ; as well may he loosen that which God hath straitened or straiten that which God hath loosened, as he may enjoin those things in religion which God hath left free, and lay on that yoke which God hath taken off.[9]

The course of events in England went on until 1689 without much regard for the opinions of these advocates of religious liberty, even though they were not isolated voices but represented, as Overton said in the title of an appeal to Parliament, "A Remonstrance of Many Thousand Citizens." The Westminster Assembly, which met by the authority of Parliament from 1643 to 1649, was designed to produce a new settlement of the Church of England in doctrine and polity by scholarly debate on the basis of Scripture, and to promote harmony with the Church of Scotland and the Reformed churches on the continent. Several able bishops were invited, but few attended because the king forbade the meeting of the assembly and most of them were loyal to him even in his declining fortunes. In any case they would have been hopelessly outnumbered, as were the handful of Independents whom the majority called the "five dissenting brethren." The assembly was 95 per cent Presbyterian in its personnel and 100 per cent so in its findings. The authorized (1647) edition of the Westminster Confession defines the Church, as Luther did, in terms of sincere personal faith and does not explicitly state that all members of the

[9] *Treatise of Civil Power in Ecclesiastical Causes* (1659).

commonwealth must necessarily be members of the one lawful Church. It does, however, affirm (Chapter XX, section IV) that the power of the civil magistrate may be invoked against any who oppose the established ecclesiastical authority or who publish erroneous opinions or maintain practices "contrary to the light of nature, or to the known principles of Christianity." (The whole confession was, of course, devoted to setting forth these "known principles.") The relation of Church and state and the function of the political power in maintaining the unity of the national church are stated more fully in Chapter XXIII, section III:

The civil magistrate may not assume to himself the administration of the Word and Sacraments, or the power of the keys of the kingdom of heaven; yet he hath authority, and it is his duty to take order, that unity and peace be preserved in the Church, and that the truth of God be kept pure and entire, that all blasphemies and heresies be suppressed, all corruptions and abuses in worship and discipline prevented or reformed, and all the ordinances of God duly settled, administered, and observed.

The restoration of the Stuarts with the return of Charles II in 1660 marked a reversal of the relative position of Presbyterians and Episcopalians in England, but no real change in the concept of a united national church and how to get it. Those who had been in were now out, and those who had been out were in. At the moment of transition there was in some minds the fleeting hope of a compromise by which the Church of England could include both. The Savoy Conference (April to July, 1661) brought together twenty-one divines of each party, but it failed completely. The Episcopalians could see no reason for compromise when it was evident that the king and the new Parliament would give them all they wanted. Within ten months both had approved a revised liturgy in which every feature of the old one that had irritated the Presbyterians was intensified, and the Act of Uniformity had been passed which immediately drove two thousand Puritan ministers from their parishes. Other punitive laws—the Five-Mile Act, the Corporation Act, the Conventicle Act, the Test Act (the last chiefly against Roman Catholics)—followed quickly to insure the complete effectiveness of the Act of Uniformity.

England again had its own national church, freed from lawful competition by any dissenting body, united in doctrine, polity, and ritual—under the patronage and protection of a Charles II. It did not, however, include the whole population. Dissenters still existed. There were no burnings of heretics or dissenters. No Puritans or Independents went to the stake, though William Penn does say that more than five thousand nonconformists died in prison within a few years. The policy was rather to starve out their clergy, to cut them off from the cultural life of the nation by exclusion from the universities, to make them second-class citizens by excluding them from civil or military office, and to reduce them to the level of social inferiority. All these purposes met with considerable success, but the main purpose failed. The dissenters did not disappear. They were not absorbed into the national church. Now freed forever from the hope of ever *being* the national church, and even from the desire to be that, they were free to move with the movement of the times toward an understanding of the meaning of civil and religious liberty, not only for themselves but for all.

As one look backs now at that crucial year of 1660, it seems that both Church and state had one of the most magnificent opportunities ever offered to any nation to take a forward step toward liberty. There were no practical reasons for repressing any man's opinions or suppressing any form of worship. From Mary Tudor to the Long Parliament, England had tried to recapture on a national scale the medieval type of unity—that is, a compulsory homogeneity of religion enforced by both civil and ecclesiastical sanctions—under each of the three forms of doctrine and polity, Roman Catholic, Episcopal, and Puritan. In the hundred years beginning with 1553 these three efforts had dismally failed. Anyone who was capable of learning anything from history or who understood the tenacity with which religious opinions are held would have known that there was no reasonable ground for the expectation that any one of these forms could wipe out the others by any measures of suppression that England would tolerate. It should have been just as obvious that none of the various existing forms of religion constituted an imminent peril to the peace and safety of the state. Roman Catholicism, to be sure, was in a violently reactionary mood in France and elsewhere; Louis XIV's barbarous dragonnades, intended to exterminate the French Huguenots, were preparing the way for the revocation of the Edict of Nantes in 1685; but there was no actual danger that Roman Catholicism would regain such a hold on England that it could proscribe other faiths and dominate the government. England had definitely become a Protestant country. The Puritans had, to be sure, beheaded a king, not because he was a king but because he was in league with the church to persecute them, but most of them had been active in promoting the return of Charles II. Even in Elizabeth's day they had not been enemies of the queen or the monarchy. John Knox's *Monstrous Regiment of Women* was aimed against Mary of Scotland and Mary of England, not against Elizabeth.

In short, the traditional belief that all forms of religious dissent were politically dangerous and socially subversive had been left entirely without factual support, if it ever had any. Every consideration of good politics, good religion, and good sense demanded the development of a type of national unity and social solidarity that would be consistent with civil and religious liberty and would therefore not be dependent on such religious homogeneity as could be secured only by penal laws against dissent. But the light had not yet dawned upon the minds of those in power.

The accession of James II, a Catholic, brought temporary relief to all dissenters. The king suspended the enforcement of all laws against both Protestant and Roman Catholic nonconformity and at the suggestion of William Penn promised full liberty of conscience and freedom of worship to all. This was scarcely a proof of the superior tolerance of Roman Catholicism. He could not get freedom for Roman Catholics except by giving freedom to all. The year in which James came to the throne (1685) was the very same year in which the Roman Catholic Louis XIV was announcing that Protestantism in France was so completely liquidated that the Edict of Nantes, which had promised them some liberties, was no longer needed. The method by which James performed his act of seeming generosity, by arbitrarily suspending acts of Parliament, was a usurpation of authority which played a part in bringing on his downfall and the end of the Stuart regime with the "bloodless revolution" of 1688.

The revolution of 1688 brought to the throne William of Orange, a Dutch Calvinist whom Hallam describes as "almost the only consistent friend of toleration in the kingdom." There were, in fact, many others, but William had the advantage of being king. The Comprehension Bill, which he urged in the first year of his reign, would have made room for all forms of church polity and for both liturgical and nonliturgical worship in one Church of England, at once more free, more united, and more nearly coextensive with the total population than it had ever been before. The bill was passed by the Lords, who were more amenable to the king's wish, but was defeated by the Commons. There was, indeed, strong opposition to it in all religious groups. All who considered that any specific system of polity and orders was established by divine authority felt compelled to oppose any arrangement that would countenance any other, and the Independents, Baptists, and Quakers could not endure episcopacy and liturgy in the same church with themselves even if these were not made mandatory for the whole Church.

The Act of Toleration, which became a law in the same year in which the Comprehension Bill failed, was the Magna Charta of dissent. It gave the right of legal existence to Presbyterians, Independents, Baptists, and Quakers. By doing so it made the Church of England explicitly and permanently the church of only a part of the nation. Roman Catholics and Unitarians were not benefited by the act. The intolerant laws of 1661-65 were left on the statute books until well into the nineteenth century, but dissenters generally were exempted from their penalties. They still labored under many civil and social disabilities. There was a heavy conservative drag upon all steps toward complete liberty and equality, and every sanction of religion was invoked to make it the heavier. The tory mind seized on the slogan "Church and Crown" to express the conviction that every relaxation of the restrictions on dissenters from the established church was an attack on the stability of the social order and an insidious undermining of the throne, and that every step toward more adequate popular representation in Parliament was an onslaught upon the church and an insult to God. The old order yielded slowly and reluctantly, even after the new order had gained a legal standing.

What was it that put an end to the inhuman persecution which had been practiced and justified as the indispensable means of preserving the unity of the total-population, "church-type" territorial church? It was neither science, reason, nor religion, said the historian George Lincoln Burr. "The pedants were as cruel as the bigots." The real antagonist of ruthlessness in the service of compulsory conformity was the "unreasoning impulse of human kindness." Even those who clung to the old idea had no longer the heart—or rather the heartlessness—to approve the measures necessary for its effective implementation. Moreover, the new order had come into concrete existence; the dissenting bodies were actually *there,* too deeply convinced of their own rightness to be persuaded and too strong to be coerced. Their historical reality had to be recognized. Part of that historical reality also was the patent fact that they were not a subversive element in the state, as the old theory had said they must be by the very fact of their nonconformity. Plain human kindness, practical politics, and pragmatic acquiescence with the inevitable have seldom collaborated more congenially than they did in this bloodless revolution in public policy concerning the nature of the visible Church and its unity. Meanwhile the theory of liberty and toleration lagged, and when it came, it was not chiefly due to the professional leaders in religion.

It must not be supposed, however, that the thinkers and theorists had nothing to do with it. They had little to do with the immediate event but much to do with its gradually widening acceptance. Most influential among them was John Locke. In the year and month of the accession of William and Mary, Locke returned from voluntary exile in the Netherlands where, like many other liberal-minded Englishmen, he had sought safety during the later years of the Stuart regime. He brought back in his baggage both the manuscript of his *Essay Concerning Human Understanding,* which was to determine the direction of English philosophy for the next century or more, and early copies of the first of his four *Letters concerning Toleration,* which had already been printed in Latin, Dutch, and French and was to be published in English the next year. Locke not only believed in the toleration of diverse religious opinions by the state as a good working arrangement in society, but he also had theories to support that belief—theories as to the nature of the Church and the field and functions of the state. He found the natures of these two institutions to be wholly different inasmuch as one is essentially a voluntary and the other a compulsory association of men, and their fields of action so distinct that neither could legitimately interfere with the other since one is concerned with the salvation of souls and the other with material interests and the preservation of civil peace and order. Doubtless he drew too sharp a line between religion and the political and social order, but the two had been so long and so disastrously confused that the emphasis needed to be laid on the separateness of their institutions.

Locke, himself a lifelong member of the Church of England, was troubled by the fact that most of those who had written in praise of toleration had wanted it only for themselves and had been ready to turn persecutor when their party was in power. Perhaps he was thinking how in the time of Charles I Puritans had escaped from the clutches of Archbishop Laud only to set up the pillory and stocks for those who dissented from their views in New England, and later had banned episcopacy in England. Or he may have thought of the Episcopalian Jeremy Taylor, Laud's protégé, who wrote his famous *Discourse of the Liberty of Prophesying* (1646) in protest against the restrictions which the then dominant Presbyterians put upon the partisans of episcopacy, quoting Tertullian, Lactantius, and all the other ancient fathers who had praised toleration when the Romans were persecuting Christians, but when his party came into power with the return of Charles II and he was made bishop of Down and Connor in north Ireland, ruthlessly ejected all the Presbyterian ministers of that region from their parishes and took possession by force.

What was needed, said Locke, was not pleas for tolerance based on self-interest but some solid principles that could be applied generally, and first of all a recognition of the true nature of the Church.

He was assuming the divine origin of the Church and the authority of Christ as mediated through the New Testament as the only guide in determining its nature when he wrote concerning the visible organization in the community or nation:

A church I take to be a voluntary society of men joining themselves together of their own accord in order to the public worshiping of God in such a manner as they may judge acceptable to him and effectual to the salvation of their souls. . . . Nobody is born a member of any church. . . . No man by nature is bound unto any particular church or sect, but everyone joins himself voluntarily to that society in which he believes he has found that profession and worship which is truly acceptable to God.

From this it follows: that the civil power is but a lawless tyranny when it forces anyone to join or not to join any particular church; that "no private person has any right in any manner to prejudice another person in his civil enjoyments because he is of another church or religion"; and that no church has "any right of jurisdiction over those that are not joined with it," even if it happens that the magistrate is of that persuasion. "And therefore peace, equity and friendship are always mutually to be observed by particular churches, in the same manner as by private persons, without any pretense of superiority or jurisdiction over one another."

Such friendly diversity of beliefs and practices would, Locke maintained, be no source of weakness to the state. On the contrary, in comparison with the desolating wars of religion and the internal broils and inhuman persecutions incident to all attempts to gain unity by compulsion, it would be a source of peace and strength. Locke was, in short, perfectly willing to sacrifice the only kind of unity the Church had had during its long history in order to gain civil and religious liberty, which he saw as two aspects of one and the same liberty, which is man's natural right.

If this, and much more in Locke's revolutionary work, now seems almost tediously obvious and axiomatic, it is, as his biographer and interpreter, A. C. Fraser, says, because its own influence "has made its argument and conclusions commonplace," so that what appeared paradoxical when he wrote it is now "the very intellectual air we breathe."

Though Locke chose division with liberty in preference to unity by compulsion, he was not willing to admit that there was not a better way than either. That better way would be for all the churches to remove the reasons for their separateness by reducing their conditions of Christian fellowship to the simple requirements for salvation as these are disclosed in the Scriptures:

But since men are so solicitous about the true church, I would only ask them here, by the way, if it be not more agreeable to the Church of Christ to make the conditions of her communion consist in such things, and such things only, as the Holy Spirit has in the Holy Scriptures declared, in express words, to be necessary to salvation; I ask, I say, whether this be not more agreeable to the Church of Christ than for men to impose their own inventions and interpretations upon others as if they were of Divine authority, and to establish by ecclesiastical laws, as absolutely necessary to the profession of Christianity, such things as the Holy Scriptures do either not mention, or at least not expressly command? Whosoever requires those things in order to ecclesiastical communion which Christ does not require in order to life eternal, he may, perhaps, indeed constitute a society accommodated to his own opinion and his own advantage; but how that can be called a *Church of Christ* which is established upon laws that are not His, and which excludes such persons from its communion as He will one day receive into the Kingdom of Heaven, I understand not.[10]

It may well be that John Locke oversimplified the problem of determining just what are those clearly defined things that can be agreed upon as "necessary to salvation" so that they may be made the sole "conditions of communion" in the churches, but it is clear that he had not forgotten the matter of peace, and even union, among the churches and that he was pointing here toward what might be a more fruitful concept than the sterile system which had been disastrously failing to produce either peace or union for more than a thousand years.

Nothing came of Locke's suggestion of a possible basis of unity among Christians; indeed, he seems to mention it almost parenthetically, or, as he says, "by the way." That path remains to be explored. The immediate effect of his work was to

[10] John Locke, *A Letter Concerning Toleration*.

reinforce the other influences that were rendering obsolete in England and all other Protestant countries the medieval concept of the Church as an institution—whether on a universal or a national scale—united in creed, cultus, and administration by the compulsive power of the state. The other influences were indeed many and in the aggregate much more potent than the words of any one man. The whole current of modern social and political thought was moving in the same direction. The spirit of liberty was on the march. By their attitudes and actions men were saying, If we cannot have liberty and a united Church, give us liberty, for a united Church without liberty is no true Church. In such a country as England, where the passion for freedom and the conservative temper exist side by side, a state church and a multitude of "free" churches could exist together, all equally free so far as voluntary membership is concerned and all exhibiting equally all the essential marks of the "sect-type church," except that the established church, which had long since ceased to be the church of the nation and was only the church of the government and a minority of the people, still carried the status it had inherited from the days when it was by force and arms the one church permitted to exist in the nation. The age of sectarianism had arrived with the age of civil and religious liberty. The agelong quest for unity had to make a fresh start from that point.

Chapter VII

The Denominational System
ECLIPSE OF THE UNITY IDEAL

A FRESH START HAD TO BE MADE IN THE QUEST FOR UNITY, but the churches were not yet ready to make it. When the irresistible advance of civil and religious liberty had rendered legal intolerance of dissent almost as odious to its former practitioners as to its victims, interest in the unity of the visible Church sank to the vanishing point in both groups. Nonconformists enjoyed their new-found sense of freedom and did the best they could under the relatively mild restrictions under which they still labored, while their sense of moral and spiritual superiority served as compensation for their status of social inferiority. Adherents of the establishment still maintained that theirs was the only real and genuine "church," all others being merely collections of "chapels"—a terminology often meekly accepted by the chapel folk—yet the manifest Christian values in the groups of nonconformists made it impossible not to recognize them as among the Christian forces of the nation and therefore as, in some sense, within the Church. So as seen from either side of the line the visible Church in the nation was actually divided, and that came to seem a normal and permanent arrangement.

In time the actual membership of the established church was reduced to a small minority of the total population. To maintain that it was still the church of the nation, defenders of that thesis were driven to the argument—seriously expressed

to me personally in 1951 by an eminent Anglican theologian—
that the Church of England is really the church of the English
people "because that is the church they stay away from when
they stay away from church." In a theological discussion Anglicans felt compelled to say that churches without a continuous
episcopate and proper "orders" could not, strictly speaking,
be churches at all or parts of the one Church. The logical inference would be that they do not represent divisions *in* the
Church but separations *from* it. Practical attitudes were not
always so rigidly logical, and they have tended to become
less so. The tendency has been toward regarding the present
arrangement as a good working system—one state church
covering the country with its network of parishes, officiating
at coronations and other public ceremonies, giving visual evidence that the government if not the whole nation is Christian, and exhibiting at least the form of that "tribal religion"
(Professor Dodd's phrase, I believe) which Christianity was
when it first conquered England; and a number of "free
churches" to accommodate those Christians who conscientiously
dissent from the distinctive position of the established church.
This is as close an approximation to the denominational system as is consistent with the existence of an establishment.

The denominational system is the same except for two
things: first, there is no establishment and no official connection of any church or churches with the government; and
second, there are no "dissenters" because there is no favored or
established church from which to dissent. In this system all
churches are free churches, all are equal before the law, all
are separated from the state, and the visible Church is frankly
and confessedly divided. Historically it has been for the most
part quite complacent about its division, glorying in the liberty
of its parts rather than seeking ways in which it might unite
them.

Since the denominational system came to its full flowering in
America, it is often regarded as a distinctively American phenomenon. There is some truth in this, though this phase

would scarcely have been possible without the previous and parallel approaches to it in England and, to a less degree, in continental Europe. The present chapter will therefore deal chiefly with the developments in America which completed that "breakdown of the medieval concept of unity" the course of which in England was traced in the preceding chapter.

The denominational system appears to be the very antithesis of a united Church. It is indeed the antithesis of the kind of unity the Church has had, or tried to have, through all the centuries since the fourth. It is for that reason the bedrock on which any enduring or endurable structure of unity must be built, or the base line from which any real advance toward that goal must be surveyed.

Far from being an American idiosyncrasy or the invention of perverse and self-willed frontiersmen in an undisciplined society detached from its cultural rootage, the sectarian pattern —which may be more politely called the denominational system—was the inevitable result of the coexistence of two old factors and one new one. The old ones have been operative in the Church for centuries; the new one came into play in the seventeenth century. All three were imported from Europe into America, where the conditions of a new society gave rise to a fourth. These four factors were: *first,* the natural rise of a variety of religious beliefs and practices; *second,* the insistence by all churches on a high degree of uniformity of beliefs and practices within their communions; *third,* the granting of religious liberty by the state; *fourth,* the entire separation between state and church. Let us look more closely at these four items.

1. The natural tendency of men's minds to develop diverse views about religion is an aspect of the more general truth that different interpretations and explanations arise in regard to everything that is not indisputably obvious—and some things that are. It is as inevitable as mutations among living organisms. It grows out of the existential fact that human beings are unique, and that the more fully human they become, the further

they are from being identical. There are different schools of medicine and philosophy, diverse views about public policy, conflicting judgments in regard to music and art. Science tends toward an ever-increasing body of certified and generally accepted knowledge—some of which may turn out to be wrong, like the centuries-long belief in the indivisibility of the atom—but it makes its advance toward unanimously accepted certainties only because it always has open frontiers of speculation and research in which explorers range far from the beaten path, invading the territory of the unknown, often by challenging what is generally supposed to be the known. In religion and philosophy, since their truths are less demonstrable than those of physics and chemistry, disagreements cannot so readily be reduced to agreements by additional research. In fact, they never have been. The history of religious thought is the history of its varieties. The labeling of some of these as "heresies" has perpetuated the memory of some that might otherwise have been forgotten. But no ecclesiastical council has ever proved that any heresy it anathematized was wrong. That is one advantage a council enjoys. It does not have to prove anything. It needs only to affirm and anathematize. But for all that, the diversity of judgments about doctrine, polity, worship, and behavior has been and continues to be a conspicuous element in the history of Christianity. Only a dreamer or a naïvely optimistic dogmatist can hope that any complete and detailed system of religious belief and behavior will ever be unanimously approved by a world of free and thinking men.

2. Churches have normally refused to allow more than a very limited scope for a diversity of views within their own communions. This was true of the Roman Catholic Church when its authority extended over central and western Europe. It was true at the same time of the Orthodox churches in the East. It was no less true of the great Protestant state churches. All these had at their command certain more or less effective means of coercion which could be applied to enforce conformity. In addition to, or as a substitute for, the enforce-

ment of conformity there was always the weapon of excommunication. The "free" churches, as they gained toleration, carried over the same basic principle of insisting upon complete homogeneity of doctrine and worship within their several communions. So in either case, whether with or without the co-operation of the state, each church (using the word now in the sense of sect or denomination) made it a point to maintain its solidarity in thought and practice. Those who did not wish to conform must be forced to conform or forced out.

3. Civil liberty arose and with it religious liberty. As the rights of man came to be more fully recognized, thanks chiefly to the work of secular thinkers and statesmen and some of the left-wing Protestants who have been mentioned, the state refused to lend its power and authority any longer for the enforcement of conformity or the punishment of nonconformity. Therefore, when the option of conforming or getting out was offered to those who dissented from a church's teaching, they *could* get out. Generally they were glad to do so, for they also were averse to having religious fellowship with any persons with whom they were not in complete agreement. Furthermore, they could without legal hindrance organize those who were like-minded with them into a new "church."

It is well to repeat at this point the statement made earlier in this book that religious liberty is simply a specific application of civil liberty and equal justice. There are special reasons why men should be concerned about freedom of conscience and the right to worship God according to the dictates of conscience without forfeiture of personal security or any of the common political, social, and economic rights of citizens; but the right to do this is implicit in any adequate recognition of human rights. The realization of this third condition therefore did not involve any radical new discovery of the special sanctity of *religious* liberty, so much as it grew out of a new recognition of the common rights of men in civil society to think, speak, persuade, publish, and organize for the dissemination of their ideas—in religion as in any other matter not

171

actually inimical to common morality and the public welfare.

When these three conditions were realized, Christianity became sectarianized. Liberty did not make it so; it merely removed the external and governmental restraints which had kept it from becoming so long before. One further step was required to turn this sectarianization into the full-blown denominational system.

4. The complete separation of church and state completed the process by putting all churches on a common level. This destroyed the illusion that in a church already sectarianized— as it was, for example, in England by the beginning of the eighteenth century—one of the sections into which it had become divided was still pre-eminently of the "church type" while all the others were "sect type." This final step was taken in America, and its result was the denominational system.

It did not happen immediately with the beginning of British colonization on the American continent. The earliest colonists in Virginia and New England brought with them the then current ideas of the necessity of religious solidarity in every political community and uniformity of doctrine and cultus in every church. One must remember when the beginnings of colonization occurred—early in the seventeenth century, when the Netherlands was the only country in Europe which came even close to tolerating dissent from its state church, and when Episcopalians and Puritans were alternately trying to control the government and ban each other in England. One must remember that the colonists themselves with few exceptions had no convictions about religious liberty, but many of them had deep convictions about the necessity of finding a place where their kind of religion could possess the field exclusively.

Not surprisingly the Puritans held to the classic views concerning toleration and heresy. As Nathaniel Ward put it in his *Simple Cobbler of Aggawam*, anyone who was willing to tolerate the active propagation of a religion other than his own was simply not sincere in it. A state that would give liberty of conscience in matters of religion might just as well give liberty of conscience in its moral laws. . . . One might (as Puritans did) close one's eyes for convenience to the deviations of some citizens who did not openly challenge the accepted way, but one could not in any case concede their right openly to divide the conscience of the community.[1]

There is no need to give many examples of the intolerance of the Puritan colonists. It is the thing best remembered about them. It is curious that among all the religious groups of their time they should be singled out by so many writers who must know better as conspicuously guilty of intolerance. For example, in his new *History of the English-speaking People,* Sir Winston Churchill comments on the Puritans of Elizabeth's time as notable for their stubborn intolerance of any religious views other than their own, apparently without noticing any tinge of the same quality in those who were evicting them from their parishes for nonconformity with *their* views and were presently to hound them out of the country for the same reason. But comparisons aside, the Puritan colonists certainly were intolerant on principle. In their view the entire community should be united in one pure Church, and intolerance of deviations was the only way to make it so.

In actual practice the idea of including the entire population in one lawful Church underwent an important and almost immediate modification. The Puritan mind was indeed firmly fixed upon the ideal of the holy state—that is, one in which the laws and customs of the community and the behavior of its citizens would conform to the law of God as they understood it. But it was deemed no less important that the church also be holy in the sense of requiring of its members some evidence of their regeneration. It was this stress upon the inner state of the soul rather than on mere conformity that set the

[1] Richard Hofstadter and W. P. Metzger, *The Development of Academic Freedom in the U.S.* (New York: Columbia University Press, 1955), p. 79. Used by permission of the publisher. For text of Nathaniel Ward's *Simple Cobbler of Aggawam* (published 1647), see Perry Miller and T. H. Johnson, eds., *The Puritans* (New York: American Book Co., 1938), pp. 226-36.

Puritans on the way toward more liberal practices. Meanwhile, only members of the church could participate in governing the colony, and only regenerate persons could be first-class members of the church. Church membership was therefore not something to be forced on the reluctant, but something for which one must qualify in order to enjoy the rights of first-class citizens. I know of no case in any colony, Puritan or other, in which punishment was inflicted or threatened for mere failure to be a member of the one authorized church. What actually was done during the first period of intolerance was: (1) to recognize only one church and permit no other; (2) to limit the franchise and the right of holding office to members of this church; (3) to enforce the regular attendance at public worship by police penalties; (4) to silence or banish active exponents of dissenting opinions or persons who might attempt to establish any other church; (5) to take rigorous measures against the disseminators of doctrines deemed especially dangerous, notably Baptists and Quakers.

In some colonies the more extreme forms of intolerance were never practiced, and in none did they continue beyond the first generation. Even in Puritan New England they did not last more than forty years after the founding of Massachusetts Bay Colony. Within that time they drove out Roger Williams, tried Anne Hutchinson, set the police on the Baptists, and burned two Quakers. By 1670 that policy had broken down, and the period of forcible suppression of nonconformity was over. The effort to keep the reins of government in the hands of church members lasted a little longer, but that too faded rapidly. The "established order" lingered on into the nineteenth century, vestigially in its later years, but dissenters of all kinds had religious liberty and full civil rights.

The classic clash was that between John Cotton and Roger Williams, representing respectively the old and the new systems. John Cotton, who was nearly fifty years old before he moved from the old Boston in Lincolnshire to the new Boston in Massachusetts, stood for the complete dominance of the

Puritan doctrine and order in the colony that his coreligionists were founding at such cost. Roger Williams, trained in law under the famous jurist Sir Edward Coke and ordained as an Anglican clergyman, had absorbed both the idea of civil liberty as the political rights of every individual and the Baptist doctrine of complete liberty of conscience as against compulsion or restraint by the state. These two convictions involved the absolute negation of the theory, reinforced by centuries of practice, that the health of state and church alike required the religious solidarity of the community. Exiled from Massachusetts after two years at Plymouth and two at Salem, he established the settlement which became Rhode Island on the explicitly avowed principle that every man's religion or lack of one was to be regarded as his own personal affair and was not in any way to affect his rights as a citizen of the commonwealth. John Cotton, the "unmitred pope of Boston," had written a tract against what he considered the dangerous idea of permitting liberty of conscience. Williams answered this argument in his *Bloudy Tenent of Persecution for the Cause of Conscience* (1644), from which a quotation was made in the preceding chapter. Cotton replied with *The Bloudy Tenent Washed and Made White in the Bloud of the Lamb.* Williams' second rebuttal was *The Bloudy Tenent yet more Bloudy.*

The conflict was between ideologies, not temperaments. John Cotton was in fact rather a kindly man, and Roger Williams seems to have been distinctly "difficult." The issue was as to the nature of the Church and its relation to the state. This issue persisted in varying forms and with diminishing intensity throughout the colonial period of American history. The intensity of the conflict diminished because the imported European theory of compulsory religious solidarity steadily lost ground and the demand for civil and religious liberty grew steadily stronger. The significant facts in the relation of all this to the origin of the denominational system are that both of these conflicting ideas about the Church existed from the

175

earliest days of the American colonies, that both were imported from Europe, and that one waned while the other waxed.

Only a few samples of the old order need be cited, and a brief reference to some familiar data on the growth of religious liberty will be sufficient.

In Virginia: A law of 1610 required church attendance on penalty of loss of a day's food allowance for the first absence, whipping for the second, six months at hard labor for the third; 1623, a fine of fifty pounds of tobacco for a month's absence from church; 1662, anyone who fails to present his infant child to a "lawful minister" for baptism is to be "amerced 2,000 pounds of tobacco"; 1663, "Quakers or other Separatists" who assemble to the number of five or more "under pretense of joining in a form of religious worship not authorized by the laws of England nor this country" are to forfeit one hundred pounds of tobacco for a first offense, five hundred for a second, and be banished for a third, and any ship master bringing any Quaker into the colony or any person allowing a Quaker to teach or preach in his house shall be fined five thousand pounds of tobacco.

In Massachusetts: 1631, the right of franchise limited to church members; 1646, a fine of five shillings for every absence from church; 1646, banishment for such "damnable heresies" as denying the immortality of the soul, the resurrection of the body, and the rightfulness of infant baptism; 1647, banishment for any Catholic priest found in the colony and death if he returns; 1651, a fine of fifty pounds or public whipping for any who deny any of the sixty-six books in the King James Version of the Bible to be "the written and infallible word of God," and banishment or death for a second offense after recantation; 1658, banishment on pain of death for members of the "cursed sect of the Quakers"; 1661, the court, desiring to use "as much lenity as may consist with our safety," softens the penalty against Quakers to require only that they "be stripped naked from the middle upwards and tied to a cart's tail and whipped through the town," and so on from one constable to the next "till they be conveyed through the outwardmost towns of our jurisdiction."

In New Amsterdam, which was presently to become New York: 1640, the charter issued by the Dutch West Indies Company declared that "no other religion shall be professed in New Netherlands except the Reformed"; Lutherans, Quakers, and Jews were not to be publicly tolerated, though Lutherans might have family prayers "each in his own home"; 1657, a citizen was fined fifty pounds for entertaining a Quaker, and a ship was confiscated for bringing one in; 1658, a Lutheran minister was sent to Holland under arrest after two Reformed ministers had protested against his coming on the ground that his admission would produce political confusion.

In New York, after it became an English possession under the patronage of the (Roman Catholic) Duke of York who became James II: 1665, the Duke's Laws broadened toleration to include the duke's coreligionists; 1683, under a Catholic governor the assembly enacted that no persons who "profess faith in God by Jesus Christ" shall be molested on account of their religion; after 1689 intolerance was directed chiefly against Catholics and especially against priests.

One cannot fail to observe that by the latter part of the seventeenth century the old struggle to suppress all dissent from the state's one authorized form of religion and to unite the entire population in one Church had been practically abandoned. It had weakened into a series of intermittent and rather halfhearted efforts to protect the community from a few particular types of religion and irreligion which seemed dangerous to public morality or to the peace and safety of the community. Dissent as such was no longer deemed an attack upon the social order. Church membership had ceased to be generally regarded as a condition of first-class citizenship, and church unity within a colony or province was seen to be not essential to the stability of the social order and in any case to be not attainable by statutory enactments and police methods.

Rhode Island and Maryland had from the beginning been

experiments in toleration. In Rhode Island it was a matter of principle, and the history of the colony was consistent with its profession. In Maryland it was a matter of policy. There is evidence that the proprietor, Lord Baltimore, a Roman Catholic, was a man of tolerant temper, but his tolerance was never put to the test. Holding his grant from a Protestant king, he could not possibly have established a colony in which Protestants would not be tolerated. His only chance of making it a refuge for Catholics was to make it open to all. The colony was started on this basis, but a little later, when Puritanism was in power in England, the Maryland Act concerning Religion (1649), though reputed to be an act of toleration, narrowed the range of permissible "liberty of conscience" to include only those who believed in Jesus Christ and the Trinity. Maryland's checkered religious history during the next century brought periods of Puritan domination, disfranchisement of Catholics, and Anglican establishment.

The first charter of the Carolinas (1663) was remarkable for the fact that, though granted to proprietors the chief of whom was a Presbyterian, Sir Ashley Cooper, and at a time when the most rigorous laws for Anglican conformity were being enacted and enforced in England, it authorized the proprietors to grant such liberty and indulgence as they pleased to any persons "who really in their judgments and for conscience' sake cannot or shall not conform to the said liturgy and ceremonies" of the Church of England. Acting under this provision, the proprietors at once instructed the assemblies of the several counties "to constitute and appoint such and so many ministers or preachers as they shall think fit and to establish their maintenance, giving liberty besides to any person or persons to keep and maintain what preachers or ministers they please." It was just a little later—but still twenty years before the writings of his *Letters Concerning Toleration*—that John Locke formulated a constitution for the Carolinas, one item of which was: "No person whatever shall disturb, molest or persecute another for his speculative opinions in religion or his way of worship." In Locke's plan the Church of England would be supported by taxation, but any seven persons might organize a church of any other kind and support it voluntarily. This draft for a constitution was never put into effect, but its ideas were those that gained acceptance in the Carolinas and in some other colonies.

Time brought rapid changes. In 1651 three visiting Baptists had been arrested and jailed in Boston, two of them heavily fined and the other publicly whipped. That was while John Cotton was still defending persecution on scriptural grounds and exchanging polemics with Roger Williams. In 1718, when the Baptist church in Boston ordained Elisha Callender, John Cotton's equally eminent grandson Cotton Mather preached the ordination sermon and his father, Increase Mather, gave the right hand of fellowship. The title of Cotton Mather's sermon, "Brethren Dwelling Together in Unity," may have been more prophetic than descriptive, but it was not absurd as it would have been in the time of his grandfather. He had the sermon printed and circulated, though he admitted that some of his friends did not like it. For his part he held that the Baptists were all wrong in their distinctive views, but that they were within their rights in holding and teaching them, because: "There is no escaping church-tyranny but by asserting the right of private judgment for every man in the affairs of his own salvation." [2]

Most of the other colonies, founded after it had been discovered in both England and America that rigid religious solidarity was as unnecessary as it was impossible, had a generous measure of toleration built into their initial charters. The Quakers in Pennsylvania were from the beginning committed to complete religious liberty and separation between church and state. Pennsylvania became a haven of refuge for many persecuted groups from Germany. Many more came there than to Rhode Island—which had similar principles and would have

[2] Quoted in Perry Miller, *The New England Mind, from Colony to Province* (Cambridge, Mass.: Harvard University Press, 1953), p. 274.

given them an equal welcome—partly because there was more room and partly because William Penn traveled in Europe preaching the Quaker gospel and inviting the distressed to migrate to his colony regardless of whether they accepted his doctrine. Meanwhile French Protestants, though forbidden to emigrate (even after the official announcement that they had been exterminated), were escaping by thousands through their country's ill-guarded frontiers and settling in the colonies all along the American coast.

Nine of the colonies which we call the "original thirteen" had established churches right up to the time of the Revolution. The religious picture in the eighteenth century was, however, quite different from that which is familiar to those who know only the European pattern of establishment. In no case did the church having official recognition by the colonial government make the slightest pretension to being the church of the entire population of the colony. In most cases it was the church of only a minority of the people. In no colony did the established church enjoy a degree of social or political prestige comparable, for example, to that of the Church of England in England. Members of dissenting groups not only had complete freedom to think and worship as they pleased and to propagate their faith, but they were free from any restriction upon their civil and political rights. By 1776 the establishments had become vestigial. The "denominational system" was on the point of arriving.

Several causes had contributed to this result. They have already been suggested, but they may now be summarized:

First, England had adopted the policy of religious toleration in 1689. In spite of the heavy drag of history and tradition the English mind had moved far and was moving farther from the ancient idea of religious solidarity at any cost. The American colonies were receiving not only a stream of immigrants but also a flow of ideas.

Second, among these ideas were those of the philosophical and cultural movement known as the Enlightenment, of which

John Locke was the first great prophet and promoter. Even those who reacted against the skeptical and secularizing aspects of this movement were drawn by it into a more critical scrutiny of time-honored institutions and practices. A philosophy of liberty was developing in England and France. England gave effect to this philosophy in its "bloodless revolution." France, where the flood of new life had been held back by Bourbon autocracy, a privileged nobility, and an entrenched hierarchy, burst the dam in a bloody revolution a century later. The American colonies accomplished this religious and cultural change against so little local resistance that their Revolution had only to "dissolve the political bands" which had connected them with the British government.

Third, in the early colonies—Virginia and New England—the second generation, preoccupied with the practical problems of wresting a living from the soil of a new country and creating institutions suitable to its conditions, was less zealous for the pure faith of their fathers and therefore less inclined to defend it by persecution, and the third was less zealous than the second. The imported idea of religious solidarity as essential to secular prosperity and political strength simply broke down in practice.

Fourth, the coming of so many immigrants of so many faiths made conformity unenforcible. So long as the phenomenon of "dissent" consisted of a radical Roger Williams teaching at Salem, or an annoying Anne Hutchinson claiming to have special revelations, or two or three bold Baptists or "vagabond Quakers" invading Boston, they could be banished or burned. But when streams of nonconformists of various kinds kept pouring into every colony and then flowing from one colony to another, the situation was radically different. Instead of remaining helpless minorities, the nonconformists in every colony became a formidable host; in most they became in the aggregate the majority.

Fifth, a surprisingly large proportion of the immigrants to colonial America were members of radical or "left-wing" Protestant sects. These were never a majority, but they were a larger minority than they had been anywhere else. They were Protestants who had either never been in one of the three great Protestant movements—Lutheran, Reformed, and Anglican—or had separated from them. Each had been a relatively feeble group in the country of its origin and so exposed to contempt as well as persecution by the church of the overwhelmingly dominant majority. Driven by that persecution, the lines of their emigration converged upon the only place where they could find freedom and land. Despised as they had been by orderly and respectable "church-type" territorial churches, they already knew in the sixteenth century or early in the seventeenth what their persecutors had to learn later, for they had learned that freedom in religion is both a civil right and an essential element in Christianity. They not only sought liberty; they believed in it. Their contribution to the developing American ideology of religious liberty can scarcely be measured.

There was one group that was an embarrassing exception to that almost universal toleration which was achieved in the American colonies. That was the Roman Catholics. Right down to the Revolution there was discrimination against Catholics in some of the colonies, and traces of this remained in some states even later. Catholic worship was forbidden in the early days in some of them; in others Catholics were disfranchised; still later, Catholic priests (or more specifically, Jesuits) were forbidden to enter under penalty of banishment or death. There were reasons for this. They are not good reasons, as we view the matter now, but they are the historical reasons. Fear and hatred of Roman Catholicism had been engendered by a long and bloody history of conflict. In England, Roman Catholics got no relief from the 1689 Act of Toleration. That the Roman Catholic Church was a foreign power claiming the right to interfere in domestic politics had been proved by the fact that the pope had declared Elizabeth "deposed" from her throne and had released her Catholic subjects from their allegiance. Protestants were being persecuted all through the seventeenth and eighteenth centuries in every Roman Catholic country in Europe. Every Roman Catholic authority from the pope down denounced the principle of religious liberty and declared that no other church but the Roman Catholic Church had a right to exist anywhere. John Locke's advocacy of toleration—an advocacy so radical that it aroused the wrath of even some Anglicans—stopped short of calling for the toleration of Catholics. They should not be tolerated, he said, because they would not tolerate others. "Where they have not the power to carry on persecution and to become masters, there they desire to live upon fair terms and preach up toleration." They demand toleration in England, said Locke, only that they may grow strong enough to take over the government and put into operation their own avowed policy of intolerance. Many of the American colonials felt the same way about it. Large numbers of them were themselves exiles from Catholic countries on account of their Protestant religion—for example, from France, from the Palatinate, from Salzburg. A large proportion of the thirty thousand Protestant Salzburgers who were "permitted" by the Prince-Archbishop to emigrate in 1731—and permitted only on urgent appeal by the king of Prussia, to save them from worse—had come to America. These things were well known throughout the colonies. However much one may deplore, as one does, that the American record is blotted by instances of intolerance, the mitigating circumstances must be remembered. It is further to be remembered, though the proof is not as easy as the citation of intolerant statutes, that before the end of the colonial period there were Catholics in all the colonies and that on the whole Catholics and Protestants were getting along together very well.

All this has been a long preparation for what needs now to be said about the denominational system in the United States. It was necessary to prevent either of two erroneous impressions —that it existed from the founding of the American colonies or that it came suddenly like a flash of inspiration at the beginning of the federal period. It was the result of a long growth. Contributing factors were: the ideas of liberty-loving Englishmen, common people, practical statesmen, theorists, and thinkers; the urge of radical reformers from continental Europe reacting to the harsh treatment they had received; the rediscovery of some simple facts about the free and voluntary character of Christianity in its earliest days—all working together on new soil and in an atmosphere in which time-honored traditions lost their sanctity and liberty seemed an essential condition of life. By the time the American colonists were ready to declare their political independence, most of them were ready also for a radical pronouncement in regard to the church.

The Virginia Declaration of Rights, adopted June 12, 1776, expressed an idea which was widely current in all the colonies and was to be a keystone of the religious policy of the nation that was about to be born. It declared:

XVI. That religion, or the duty which we owe to our Creator, and the manner of discharging it, can be directed only by Reason and Conviction, not by force or violence; and therefore all Men are equally entitled to the free Exercise of Religion, according to the dictates of Conscience; and that it is the mutual duty of all to practice Christian Forbearance, Love and Charity, towards each other.

Ten years later the Virginia Act for Establishing Religious Freedom, written by Thomas Jefferson and adopted January 16, 1786, went still further. The 1776 statute had freed the consciences but not the purses of citizens from compulsion by the state on behalf of the church. The 1786 act laid down these principles: (1) that the state has no right to compel the citizen to support with his money the propagation of any religious opinions, even his own, much less those in which he does not believe; (2) that "civil rights have no dependence on our religious opinions," so that no civil disability could be laid upon any person by reason of his religious belief or affiliation; (3) that eligibility to public office ought not to be conditioned upon the profession or renunciation of any religious opinion (a mere development of the implications of the preceding point); (4) that all men are free to worship as they will or not to worship at all without restraint or penalty; and (5) that all are equally "free to profess, and by argument to maintain, their opinion in matters of religion"—which would include even antireligious opinions. Note that the first of these pieces of legislation in Virginia was enacted less than a month before the Continental Congress adopted the Declaration of Independence, and the second the year before the Constitutional Convention of 1787.

The effect of the second Virginia act was not only to disestablish the Episcopal Church but to reject decisively the proposal, strongly urged by some honored and influential men, that Christianity in general should be declared the "religion of the state" and that church taxes, collected by the state, should be distributed among the churches as the persons who paid them might designate. In this way the ministers of all denominations would be supported by public funds. There was a real battle on this point. The debate got a great deal of publicity in Virginia and elsewhere. The sweeping action which brought about complete separation of church and state was not taken by inadvertence. The plan of giving all churches equal treatment and having them all related to the state by supporting them all by taxation was an unusual but not an unprecedented arrangement. It was, in fact, actually in operation in South Carolina at the very time when the proposal was being debated and rejected in Virginia, for the South Carolina constitution of 1778 had listed all the churches then represented there and had declared them all collectively to be the "established church of this state," and had specified the ways in which ministers should be certified and supported and other churches admitted to the same status as they appeared on the scene.

All this was perfectly well known to the members of the

Constitutional Convention which framed the Constitution of the United States in 1787, and to the members of the first Congress when only three years later they voted to submit for ratification the First Amendment to the Constitution.

The First Amendment declared that "Congress shall make no law respecting an establishment of religion." In the light of the Virginia debates and the South Carolina constitution, both of which were matters of common knowledge, the First Amendment was clearly intended to mean: no federal establishment of any one church; no establishment of several or all churches by levying a tax to be distributed equitably among them; in short, no law whatsoever looking toward the establishment or support of religion by the government. Other phrases in the same amendment forbidding abridgment of the rights of free speech, publication, and assembly further guaranteed the exercise of religious liberty. The phrase "separation of church and state," coined later, correctly described the situation produced and guaranteed by the First Amendment.

The choice of any one church to be given preferred status as the established church of the nation would, of course, have been politically impossible. No one church had a majority of the nation's people among its supporters. It is doubtful whether any that were established churches in late colonial days, or remained established in certain states after 1789, had the support of a majority even in the colonies or states in which they had that status. The nation as a whole was a complex of religious minorities, the most numerous of which was almost certainly outnumbered by the next two. Since the dawn of Christianity no people had ever begun its national life under those conditions. The establishment of a church of the nation or of the government would have been impossible. The men who framed the Constitution and the First Amendment, and the constituencies which ratified them, are not on that account entitled to the less credit. They had participated in the total movement of thought which made the new order of complete religious liberty for individuals and complete legal equality for all

186

communions no less desirable in the eyes of the American people generally than it was politically and socially inevitable.

The adoption of separation of church and state as a constitutional principle of the American government completed the development of the denominational system as a pattern of church life and fixed its relation—or rather its lack of any relation—to any help or hindrance that it might receive from the civil government. It remained to be seen how the churches would develop under that system and what would be their attitudes toward one another now that all were free and legally equal.

Since the main theme of this book is the changing concepts of unity, it must be said first of all that the ideal of unity suffered an almost complete eclipse. It is true that some theologians, reflecting upon certain texts touching upon the relation between Christ and the Church, felt constrained to say that the Church considered as the mystical body of Christ must necessarily be one body, but this implied nothing as to any visible and functional unity among the many sects into which believers were now fortunately free to divide. Certain denominations were able to find all the unity they were interested in by assuming that they alone were the true Church, that all others lacked some element of true churchliness and so were no part of the Church, and that therefore the true Church was not divided. This was essentially a revival of the third-century process of attaining unity by exclusion. It can be practiced by a small sect as easily as by a large group that calls itself the "Catholic Church." Most of the American denominations, however, simply lost sight of the ideal of unity and lived happily in their divided state, rejoicing in their new-found freedom, recognizing one another as groups of worthy but more or less erring Christians, and each seeking its own aggrandizement as the best way to promote the triumph of truth and the coming of the kingdom of God.

It was from this frank and often friendly, but generally complacent, sectarianism that the American churches had to take off for any possible future advance toward ecumenicity.

Though the situation was one of competition in an open field, the relations among churches were not necessarily hostile. The field was large. It was a new country with an open frontier into which population was pouring at such a rate that all churches had room for expansion. Less than 10 per cent of the total population of the United States were members of any church at the time of the first federal census. (The figure is more often put at 7 per cent.) Competition in new communities sometimes led to lively clashes, but on the whole the friendliness of the frontier prevailed.

Two contrasting features of denominationalism in America have been: first, the increasing number of denominations; and second, the movement toward co-operation and unity among them.

Visitors from Europe frequently mention the multiplicity of sects as the first feature of the religious scene that strikes their attention. This condition is deplorable, but its explanation is not too discreditable. America has more sects than any other country because: (1) In receiving immigrants from all countries, it received members of all the sects that any of them had and many of them as refugees. (2) Successive waves of immigrants of the same general faith (for example, Lutheran and Reformed) retained their separateness on national, linguistic, and confessional lines. (3) The absence of legal restraints or civil disabilities gave free scope to divisive movements. (4) The general relaxation of the sense of being under authority and a tendency to independent thought and action—precious but dangerous features of a relatively new society in a free country—acted as a centrifugal force in organized religion. Many ecclesiastical mutations and separatist movements arose from a revival of the early Protestant principle of direct appeal to the Bible as the sole authority in religion together with the conviction that any plain man could understand it. In view of the low level of theological and biblical education (even among those who became familiar with the words of many

188

texts of Scripture), it was easy for amateur theologians to seize upon some selection of passages and make their interpretation of these the basis for a new communion. Meanwhile the older denominations for the most part stood fast by the requirement of such a degree of conformity to their doctrinal standards and their church practices that persons of variant views found it uncomfortable, if not impossible, to remain in communion with them.

All these factors contributed to raising the number of separate denominations in the United States to the astounding number of 268, according to the 1956 listing. Although the majority of these are splinter sects whose aggregate membership is an almost negligible fraction of the whole, and although more than three fourths of the Protestant Christians in the United States can be classed as either Baptists, Methodists, Lutherans, or Presbyterians, the proliferation of sects in America is still a conspicuous and sobering fact. The question at once arises as to the attitudes of these sects toward one another and their effect on the prospects for unity.

As a rough generalization, subject to many exceptions, it may be said that the relations among the denominations were generally friendly and often co-operative during the first third of the nineteenth century; that divisions multiplied and sectarian acrimony increased during the second third; and that there was a revival of amity and co-operation in the last third, preparing the way for many denominational reunions and for the more comprehensive ecumenical movement which began approximately with the twentieth century.

It would not serve our present purpose to recite in any detail the many expressions of unitive thought and the many forms of co-operative action by American churches during the nineteenth century. Readers are referred to other recent books which treat this topic more or less fully.[3] It would, however,

[3] Ruth Rouse and Stephen C. Neill, eds., *A History of the Ecumenical Movement* (Philadelphia: Westminster Press, 1954), pp. 221-59. W. E. Garrison, *Christian Unity and Disciples of Christ* (St. Louis: Bethany Press, 1955), pp. 32-79.

be misleading to leave the record of that century blank and so permit the impression that it was wholly negative in relation to the unity of the Church. To fill this gap it may be useful to include at least an unannotated list of movements and events which looked in the direction of unity. Most though not all of these were co-operations of individuals belonging to many churches rather than of the churches themselves, and their purpose was collaboration in common tasks rather than the uniting of churches. Nevertheless they all presupposed that the separated churches were in truth parts of one Church and partners in the Christian enterprise, and they demonstrated the possibility of Christian fellowship across the denominational frontiers. Here then is such a bare list:

The Great Western Revival, in which Presbyterians, Methodists, and Baptists collaborated, 1800 and a little after.

The foreign missionary movement, especially the American Board of Commissioners for Foreign Missions, 1810, Congregational, Presbyterian, and Dutch Reformed (not wholly Congregational until 1870).

The American Bible Society, 1816, Presbyterians, Congregationalists, Episcopalians, Baptists, Methodists, Dutch Reformed, and Friends.

Many undenominational societies for the publication and distribution of tracts, for the promotion of Christian education, the assistance of students for the ministry, the abolition of slavery, the encouragement of temperance, and other moral, humanitarian, or religious purposes, 1820-50.

The Sunday-school movement, undenominational until about 1832, as illustrated by the New York Sunday School Union, 1816, and the American Sunday-School Union, 1824. Then, after a period of denominational separateness the new International Sunday School Association, which adopted the plan of uniform lessons in 1872 and provided a massive exhibition of interdenominational co-operation.

The irenic proposals of S. S. Schmucker, Lutheran, whose

Fraternal Appeal to the American Churches, With a Plan for Catholic Union, on Apostolic Principles (1838) was often reprinted and widely read.

The Young Men's Christian Association, organized in England in 1844, came to America in 1855 and had phenomenal growth. It was soon followed by the Young Women's Christian Association. Out of these grew the Student Christian Movement and the Student Volunteer Movement for Foreign Missions, to which American churches made important contributions of personnel and leadership.

The Evangelical Alliance, London, 1846, was predominantly British, but one tenth of its membership was American. The American branch was formed in 1867.

Plans for the reunification of the whole Church by Episcopalians Thomas Hubbard Vail (1841), William Augustus Muhlenberg (1853), and William Reed Huntington (1870).

The rise and growth of the Disciples of Christ, who from their earliest pronouncements in 1804 and 1809 made the unity of the Church their avowed objective.

The Chicago Quadrilateral basis for reunion, issued by the Episcopal General Convention (1886), approved with slight amendment by the Lambeth Conference.

The Young People's Society of Christian Endeavor, 1881.

The Foreign Missions Conference of North America, a consultative organization of denominational mission boards, 1893.

The twentieth century has witnessed accelerated advance into other fields of co-operation and bold adventures in the direction of organic unity. To continue our bare listing of significant movements and events:

Formation of the Federal Council of the Churches of Christ in America, 1908.

The organization of the International (U.S. and Canada) Council of Religious Education, 1922, by the merger of two earlier interdenominational organizations and its immense growth in scope and influence.

The union of the Federal Council, the International Council, and six other agencies to form the National Council of Churches, 1950.

The formation of a vast number of city, county, and state councils of churches covering almost every part of the country.

Organizations for the promotion of peace, such as the Church Peace Union and the World Alliance for Promoting International Friendship through the Churches.

The Faith and Order Movement, having its origin in almost simultaneous proposals in the conventions of two American denominations in 1910.

Thirteen completed denominational unions or reunions in the first half of the twentieth century, as compared with none in the thirty-six years following the reunion of Old School and New School Presbyterians in 1870.

The formation of the United Church of Canada, 1925, comprising Methodists, Presbyterians, and Congregationalists in a neighboring country having a denominational system identical with that of the United States.

The Philadelphia Plan of union, formulated by a conference called by the Presbyterians in 1918, never ratified by any of the participating denominations but a significant sign of the urge toward unity.

The Greenwich Plan, growing out of a conference initiated by the Congregationalists and seconded by the Disciples of Christ in 1949 and still a live issue for the eight participating bodies and others.

The E. Stanley Jones Plan for a federal union of denominations.

The purpose of this bare listing of unitive movements in America is to indicate and to prove that the denominational system in actual practice has not been the complete antithesis to Christian unity that it may seem to those who have in mind only the statistical fact that there are 268 denominations in the United States or who think only of the conditions they may have observed in some town that has six starving churches where it could not decently support more than one good one. It does, to be sure, exhibit the visible Church in a state of extreme and lamentable fragmentation. But it also shows the churches—or if the phrase seems more accurate, these fragments of the Church—shorn of some illusions that have haunted the territorial churches for ages. These fragments know that they are fragments. Few of them still cherish the fallacy that they and they alone *are* the Church. With confidence in the rightness of their own system of doctrine and order and zeal for its propagation, some will not co-operate with other bodies in any good work, but only a marginal minority even of these regard the bodies with which they will not co-operate as wholly outside of Christ's Church. Churches in the denominational system are wholly voluntary in their membership and wholly free from either restraint or support by the civil government, as any conceivable united Church in the modern world must be. They have, in short, stripped themselves of most of the encumbrances which in other times and places rendered impossible the free and honest union of all Christians in one Church even when the demand for unity was most insistent and the means employed for attaining it were most vehement.

The denominational system with all its odious features embodies some elements which are essential to unity in the modern world. Chief of these are complete religious liberty for individuals and freedom of action and equality of status for churches. Its extreme divisiveness, growing out of recognition of the right to divide, implies also the right to unite and makes it the logical starting point for advance toward a unity that free men can freely accept. That advance has already begun. How far it will go depends upon the ability and willingness of the denominations to learn still another lesson about Christian freedom.

Chapter VIII

The Ecumenical Awakening
THE CHARACTER OF A UNITED CHURCH

LET US NOW TRY TO SEE WHETHER THE STORY OF THE CHURCH'S long quest for unity means anything to us as we face the problem in our own time. It is only partly true that the "only thing we learn from history is that we learn nothing from history." That is true in the sense that it is true for some people. There is a type of mind that delights in stubbornly driving up blind alleys which history has clearly marked with the sign "No Thoroughfare." Where this attitude prevails, there is of course nothing to be learned from history—and no progress to be made in the present or future. Our hope must be that this attitude will not generally and permanently prevail. Let us again summarize what has been said in the preceding chapters.

The unity that has been sought throughout almost the entire course of Christian history after its earliest age is a unity requiring conformity to a standardized body of theology, uniformity in modes of worship, and acceptance of a specific type of organization generally having a centralized authority.

The scope of the unity sought has been successively (1) the whole Church throughout the world, (2) the church within a single nation or other territorial unit of civil government, and (3) the denomination. The word "church" has come to be used in these three meanings.

The normal method for trying to achieve and maintain unity

has varied according to the scope of the "church" concerned and its relation with the civil power. (1) When the unity of the whole Church was the aim, the procedure passed through two phases: *First,* before the Church gained legal status and political power, it practiced the exclusion of those who varied from the standards of doctrine and practice approved by the majority, branding them as "heretics" but having no weapon against them except excommunication and maintaining its unity by declaring that the Church consisted only of those who conformed. *Second,* after the Church made alliance with the state, Church and state together applied compulsion to secure universal conformity to the standards approved by both authorities and enforced it by whatever forms of pressure and violence seemed most likely to be effective.

(2) When the nation was the unit, the police power of the state was still available for coercion and the method was still compulsory conformity, but now necessarily on a nation-wide rather than a (theoretically) world-wide scale. The rigors of persecution were, however, alleviated by the possible alternatives of banishment or escape to another governmental area. The irresistible rise of civil liberty and growing respect for the rights of man in Protestant countries rendered it impossible to maintain national religious unity by compulsion and persecution, which were the only means that had ever been even approximately effective.

(3) With the consequent appearance of legalized or partly legalized free denominations alongside of the established church—which had itself become a denomination in spite of its pretension to a superior "churchly" character—each of these denominations had the task of preserving its own unity. For this purpose they fell back upon the most ancient method in this series, namely, the exclusion of deviates from their respective systems of doctrine, worship, and polity. Since this method did not involve any reliance upon co-operation by the state, it passed over without essential modification into the completed denominational system as exhibited in the United States.

That this is an oversimplified diagrammatic representation of the history of the Church in its quest for unity does not detract from the essential accuracy of the picture. The degree of permissible variation in doctrine, cultus, and polity has varied from time to time. Always there has been some margin of liberty in matters which the Church had not yet reduced to rule or in which it thought variety was harmless. At times this margin has been fairly wide, at other times uncomfortably narrow. At worst, no church has ever been quite "totalitarian." The demand for conformity was never absolute and all-embracing; but always it covered large areas of doctrine, worship, and polity, and in these the demand was absolute. In some modern denominations (for example, Congregationalists and Disciples of Christ) the requirement of doctrinal uniformity has weakened to the point where it has almost vanished. In others (for example, Lutherans) it is maintained with some strictness. In most it is applied chiefly to the clergy, and there is little scrutiny to see whether laymen are doctrinally sound or not.

The techniques of compulsion were never completely effective even when the Church viewed the burning of its heretics without shame or compunction. Not all heretics were burned. Some were not even silenced. Administration was often slack. Ecclesiastics had other interests which took their attention away from the liquidation of heresy. Sometimes a religious rebel had the protection of a powerful political friend, as Wycliffe had of John of Gaunt.

All these exceptions must be taken into account to prevent the generalized picture from being a caricature, but it is true as a general picture. The Mississippi River flows toward every point of the compass at one part or another of its long course, yet one does not distort geography in saying that in a general way it flows south. So the course of history has not followed an undeviating line according to the formula given above or any other formula. Yet it has on the whole flowed in the direction indicated. The Church has clung tenaciously to the idea that its unity, or the unity of its parts, demanded a high degree of uniformity. It has tried to get this unity of uniformity by burning, banishing, or silencing dissenters when it had the power, and by excommunicating them and declaring them no part of the Church when it did not have the power to coerce or had become too squeamish or too civilized to persecute. There have been no other ways of getting that kind of unity.

While these methods of attaining conformity were being practiced with greater or less temporary success, all the arts of argument and persuasion were also being used, but to little effect. It is true that the Inquisition never encumbered its proceedings by engaging in theological debate with its intended victims, but it was an extreme case. Controversy and discussion have played a conspicuous part in the history of Christian thought. Every point that is now an article in any creed was once an item on the agenda of a church council, and the debate was not ended by the council's decision. The total mass of theological discussion that has been piled up in manuscript and print from the third century until now is staggering in quantity, not to mention the even greater mass of oral argument. In the aggregate these presentations of diverse views have had great value, but they have never been relied upon to produce a solid doctrinal consensus and they have never produced it. Any who think that theological agreement can now be reached by a few more conferences and commissions and "study groups" may profitably remember that this method has been tried continuously for centuries and that the net result has been the proliferation of diverse opinions now strongly held by devoted and presumably intelligent Christians.

The whole point of the historical survey which has occupied the greater part of this book is to suggest the necessity of re-examining a concept of unity (1) which the Church has never been able to bring to actuality by argument and persuasion; (2) which broke down when it was partially realized by violence, compulsion, and such disregard of elementary human rights as modern men will not endure and Christian men never should have countenanced; and (3) which, when carried over into an age which had rejected violence as a means of suppressing religious diversity, resulted only in a sectarian solidarity that is the very antithesis of a united Church.

Throughout this discussion our thought has been oriented toward nothing less than the unity of the whole Church. Before proceeding further to consider what kind of unity is either conceivably possible or desirable for the whole Church, we must make a clear distinction between this objective and that of uniting two or more related or congenial denominations. These two kinds of union are radically different and require quite different approaches.

During the past fifty years at least thirteen mergers of particular denominations have been consummated, and others are on the way. Some of these have been reunions of bodies once united or of groups having a common denominational background of doctrine and polity; others, the merging of denominations which have reached similar positions by different routes. Every such merger rests upon a "basis of union" which recognizes a sufficient body of common doctrine to satisfy the parties concerned, provides by compromise or otherwise for a single acceptable form of polity and a relatively uniform mode of worship if these did not previously exist among the contracting denominations, and arranges for the consolidation of their missionary, educational, and publishing agencies. The result is that the united group usually has about the same degree of uniformity in doctrine and practice that each of its constituents had before their union.

Illustrations of the various phases of this process will readily come to mind as one thinks of recent or prospective denominational unions. In the merging of Lutheran bodies, the most serious problem has been to formulate a confession of faith that would be acceptable to all, though all were already strictly within the Lutheran tradition. In the Presbyterian union of 1957 there is no question but that the resultant standard of doctrine and system of polity will be as thoroughly Presbyterian as they were in the uniting churches. The union of Methodists, Presbyterians, and Congregationalists to form the the United Church of Canada was remarkable in that it involved churches with three different types of polity and required a compromise among them as well as a relaxation of some doctrinal standards that had previously been cherished. The still more remarkable Church of South India, which included episcopal as well as nonepiscopal bodies, is chiefly interesting in this connection for its compromise on polity and "orders" and as an illustration of Anglican patience, for the terms of the compromise are such that this church will be thoroughly episcopalized within thirty years from the date of its organization.

Among the pending proposals for the union of specific denominations, the most ambitious is what is called the "Greenwich Plan." Eight Protestant bodies, including some very large ones, have participated in the conferences which began at Greenwich, Conn., in 1949 and in the preparation of a draft for a basis of union among them. The initial call was for a meeting of representatives of denominations which recognized the validity of one another's ministries and sacraments. In scanning the whole range of denominations which would have to be united in a completely united Church, it is easy to see that some present more serious obstacles to union than others and that one of the principal obstacles is the lack of mutual recognition of ministries and sacraments. It would seem that union among those without this impediment might become an accomplished fact long before the slower process of rapprochement among those still divided on the validity of "orders" and sacraments could reach a culmination. The promoters of the Greenwich Plan acted on the slogan "Let those unite who will unite"—a principle somewhat analogous to the principle of "Reformation without tarrying for any" upon which the early English Independents acted. At least it meant an effort to proceed with the union of the denominations which could be most easily united without tarrying for those who, though perhaps just as eager for union, were more insistent that it should be upon their own terms. The actual proposals under the Greenwich Plan, though drafted and discussed at more than one conference, are not yet in final form for submission to the participating denominations. It is apparent, however, that the proposed basis of union, though relatively free in its doctrinal requirements (almost completely untheological in its earliest form) and flexible in regard to modes of worship, will include a definite and integrated system of polity incorporating elements of the Methodist, Presbyterian, and Congregational systems.

These are all commendable movements, tending to reduce the number of competing denominations and increase the effectiveness of the Christian enterprise in their respective areas, and exhibiting the spirit of Christian fellowship. None of them is a "pilot project" which can serve as a pattern for a union of the whole Church. Always they call for compromises which many conscientious Christians and some whole communions cannot accept. Nearly always they leave on the outside considerable groups—witness the continuing Presbyterians and Baptists in Canada, and the communions in South India that do not want to be episcopalized even thirty years later.

The distinction is often made between "giving up" something and "contributing" something when denominations come together in a union. It is a valid and valuable distinction and it applies equally to a union of two or three denominations and to a union of the whole Church. Serious and conscientious Christians are not going to "give up" anything except their separateness as the price of uniting with other Christians, except perhaps under pressure of some local emergency. Any long-range and full-scale scheme of union based upon the idea of "giving up" is foredoomed to failure from the start.

The correlative question is, What does it mean to "contribute" something to a united Church? It might mean to contribute some item of doctrine or polity, hitherto belonging distinctively to the contributing group, with the expectation or demand that henceforth it shall be mandatory for the whole united body. In some actual mergers it has meant exactly this, and in mergers of two or three congenial denominations it may work well enough. But it is obvious that this kind of "contributing" by one of the uniting parties requires that the others shall "give up" whatever would not harmonize with this contribution. In contrast with this, to contribute might mean that each constituent element of a merger would come into it bringing its own beliefs and practices and contributing these to the common store that would be at the disposal of all but would be forced upon none. Such a union would certainly not exhibit uniformity of doctrine, worship, or polity. It might produce harmony, fellowship, mutual aid in seeking more truth, and more co-operation than we now have in the promotion of the whole Christian enterprise. It could do so if those who "contribute" some cherished practice or emphasis would refrain from regarding the failure of others to adopt it as a breach of unity and a barrier to fellowship.

It is probable that most Christians who are interested in unity would like to see a united Church that would be an enlarged replica of their respective denominations, or such a union as would be produced if all others came to their position. It is not surprising, and it should not be disillusioning, if this is true. Such a desire is undergirded by the history of the several communions and the loyalties that have been built around them. Who among us has not been nourished on the conviction that our church is "right" and that other churches have only such a limited degree of rightness (mingled with error) as results from some accidental overlapping of their positions with ours? It is often stated as an axiom in ecumenical circles that only a "union on the truth" can be valid or enduring. Well, then, if "we" have the truth, it must follow as the night the day that union is possible only on "our" position.

Accordingly, Lutherans would like to have a united Church which would sanction such definitions of doctrines and sacraments as are provided in the Augsburg Confession. Presbyterians would like to have a presbyterial polity and a doctrinal system approximating that of the Westminster Confession. Episcopalians have frequently been heard to say that they will have nothing to do with a united Church that does not have its entire clergy ordained by bishops standing in unbroken lineal succession from the apostles, and the Church of England is not yet in communion with the Church of South India because it has not up to this time completely fulfilled that requirement. Disciples of Christ, who came into existence as advocates of union and have never ceased to regard it as a major objective, have generally envisaged a united Church as one in which "faith, repentance, and baptism" (by immersion) would be the terms of admission, and which would universally employ such "apostolic" practices as the weekly observance of the Lord's Supper, a nonliturgical form of worship, a minimal degree of distinction between ministry and laity, and complete congregational independency. Baptists, who have been as little interested in unity as any, might consider it if they were assured that "believers' baptism" would be the rule and separation between Church and state, complete religious liberty, and congregational autonomy the universal practice.

Such attitudes, if maintained, would simply bring the whole movement for a united Church to a deadlock and a standstill. These groups and others have been trying for centuries to convert one another to their respective positions, but there has been little progress. They have all won many converts from among the unchurched, and there have been so many of the unchurched in America that the denominations have flourished and grown. Their converts from one another have approximately balanced. Transfer of membership from one denomination to another has become a familiar feature of American church life, but the reasons are generally personal, social, geographical, or purely incidental. No single denomination has a rational or statistical ground for expecting that it will "take the world" to the exclusion of all others or bring all the others to rally under its banner by the force of its arguments or the power of its propaganda. Among the things that history teaches to those who are capable of learning anything is that this road to unity is closed—or more accurately, does not exist.

Minor concessions on items not held with deep conviction may produce compromise platforms upon which two or more denominations can stand together as one. This is good, so far as it goes; but if the body formed by such a merger stands on this platform as firmly as the parties to it stood on their former platforms, and uses it as the criterion of its fellowship, there has been no real progress toward a united Church. Unity will not come by having bigger, better, fewer, and more complacent sects.

Open-minded students have recently discovered that some of the differentiating features of the several communions have taken form under the influence of "nontheological factors" in their cultural situations. This fact has, indeed, long been a matter of common knowledge, but there has come to be a new understanding of its significance. Much attention was given to this subject at the Third World Conference on Faith and Order at Lund, Sweden, in 1952, and at a smaller preparatory conference a year earlier.[1] Some fresh and stimulating insights have come from this approach, since it invites every stout defender of a specific pattern of doctrine and practice to face the question as to how much of it carries the stamp of the divine authority he has been in the habit of ascribing to it and how much was determined by secular environmental influences. The various Christian groups have never been hesitant about discovering secular ingredients and determinants in one another's positions; the novelty lies in the application of a similar scrutiny to one's own.

In so far as tenets that have been regarded as grounds for

[1] For a much earlier treatment of topics in this field see J. T. McNeill, Matthew Spinka, and Harold R. Willoughby, eds., *Environmental Factors in Christian History* (University of Chicago Press, 1939), a volume of essays in honor of Shirley Jackson Case, who was a pioneer in this area of research.

separation come to be held with some degree of elasticity for this or other reason, compromise becomes easier and the range of possible denominational mergers is widened. This improves the immediate situation and therefore deserves encouragement; but it is not even an approach to the main goal, which is a united Church. There is a limit to the explanation of ecclesiastical differences on the ground of nontheological factors. In any case, the union of Christians is not going to be attained by whittling away the convictions that now divide them.

The question is not whether Christians must have convictions. The question is whether all the Christians in any one "church," or in the future united Church, must have the same convictions. The insistence that they must, on all matters on which the church has made a pronouncement, has been the root of most of our divisions. And yet, in spite of the traditional demand for doctrinal homogeneity within each section of the Church, diversities have crept in. Since scholars began to study the Bible by scientific and historical methods and since the rise of the theological movements of the last hundred years, the lines between denominations have ceased to coincide with those between the types of theology. Every religious group that has not closed its frontiers against the importation of ideas, whether liberal or conservative, now harbors fairly wide varieties of doctrine. Some denominations contain within themselves almost as wide a range of theological opinion and biblical interpretation as can be found in the whole body of contemporary Christian thought. It is a good omen, but it does not mean that the denominations are ready to throw down their walls and let Christians unite in spite of their differences. At every conference that looks toward a merger, the "basis of union" becomes a controversial issue.

The Roman Catholic view of the requirements for a united Church is perfectly clear. It has been authoritatively stated scores of times, and no generous and fraternal phrases uttered by fine-spirited priests or laymen (of whom there are many) can alter the position of their church in the slightest degree.

Pope Pius XI in his encyclical *Mortalium Animos* voiced his opposition to "schemes for the promiscuous union into one body of all who call themselves Christians," and continued: "Federation of Christians then is inconceivable in which each member retains his own opinions and private judgments in the matter of faith. . . . Unity can arise only from one teaching authority, one law and belief and one faith of Christians." This statement is perfectly consistent with the history and principles of a church which, holding the clear-cut concept here expressed that unity requires complete conformity, applies one or the other of the only two techniques by which that kind of unity can be attained—police methods when it can or, when that is impossible, the declaration that the Church consists only of those who do conform to the requirements of its centralized authority and so by definition can never be divided.

It appears to be true that a large proportion of the present-day Protestant leaders who are active in the ecumenical movement believe that an approximate uniformity of doctrine, polity, and worship is essential to "full unity" and cherish the hope that it can be attained by theological study and conference. Beneath this lies the sense of a deeper unity, too vague to be visible but furnishing the real motive for the whole enterprise. In ecumenical gatherings the statement "We are all one in Christ" is so frequently repeated that it has become almost a refrain. Nothing truer could be said. In so far as we are one, we are one in Christ. But the temptation is almost irresistible to move away from this majestic simplicity by seemingly logical inferences to conclusions that are far apart and thoroughly divisive when taken as criteria of fellowship or requirements of a united Church. For example:

We are all one in Christ. Christ gave authority to his apostles and authorized them to appoint their successors, who are bishops. Therefore a united Church must have bishops in unbroken succession from the apostles, and such bishops and a clergy ordained by them are essential to the reality and genuineness of the Church.

We are all one in Christ. Christ commanded his apostles to baptize (immerse) all nations, and the apostles demanded faith and repentance as conditions of baptism. Therefore a united Church must consist only of penitent and believing persons who have been immersed on profession of their personal faith.

We are all one in Christ. Christ blessed the little children and said, "Of such is the kingdom of heaven." Peter, speaking for Christ, said, "The promise is to you and to your children," and Paul baptized whole households, and baptism "came in place of circumcision." Therefore the family is the unit, and the church must include baptized (sprinkled) believers and their baptized children.

We are all one in Christ. Christ said that the Holy Spirit will "guide you into all truth." The truth into which the Holy Spirit guided the apostles and the Church includes the theology implicit in Paul's epistles and the definitions of the Trinity and the nature of Christ as expressed in the creeds of the ecumenical councils and one or more of the great Reformation confessions. Therefore the Church must have a sound doctrinal foundation conforming to these classic statements.

The list could be indefinitely extended. These are not formulas for union. True or false as exegetical or theological pronouncements, they are ways of perpetuating division if they are used as criteria of fellowship. Not all Christians think there is historical evidence that Jesus gave any such authority to his apostles or to bishops as their successors. Some who reject the alleged historical and theological grounds for regarding bishops as essential to the very existence of the Church would for themselves accept the episcopate as a good administrative arrangement but could not be parties to unchurching those Christians who would not. Some who approve of believers' baptism by immersion realize that scholarly opinion is not unanimous, so would refuse to exclude those sprinkled in infancy or to allow any opinion about baptism to be a condition of union or a barrier to it. Some who believe all the classic creeds would refuse to say that all Christians must or to regard them as permanent standards of orthodoxy to which the Church must adhere as the "symbols" and "witnesses" of its faith. To make any of these things essential characteristics of the Church is to perpetuate the spirit—if not the damnatory phraseology—of the *Quicumque vult,* which is not the basis of a united Church but is a divisive heresy.

The Faith and Order Movement has performed a magnificent service in bringing together serious and responsible thinkers representing many communions in many nations. In three world conferences on Faith and Order, in many smaller conferences and sessions of standing committees during the twenty years since Edinburgh in 1937, and now in its continuing activities as a commission within the World Council of Churches, it has provided opportunity for frank and fraternal discussion of the most fundamental questions, including those which have furnished the grounds of separation among the churches.

The first possible result of such conferences is that the participants may come to a better understanding of one another's positions and the reasons for holding them. This result has been actual as well as possible.

A second possible result could be the growth of attitudes of mutual esteem and affection and a warm sense of Christian fellowship reaching across even the widest theological chasms. This has actually happened to a degree not easily realized by any who have not been personally involved in these friendly encounters over a long series of years. In these conferences there has been a meeting of hearts, if not of minds, and the saying that "we are one in Christ" has had a poignant meaning.[2]

[2] I cannot refrain from giving this testimony based on my own personal experience, which includes participation in the world conferences at Oxford, Edinburgh, Amsterdam, Lund, and Evanston, a ten-day meeting of the Theological Commission on the Church at Cambridge, England, and one on "nontheological factors" at the Chateau de Bossey, Switzerland, and the semiannual two- or three-day meetings of the American Theological Committee over a period of about ten years.

A third conceivable outcome of such prolonged and profound discussions by Christian scholars, all sincerely devoted to the discovery of truth, might be that they would come to unanimous agreement on the matters considered. But no such result has followed. The diversity of convictions about doctrines, church polity, forms of worship, and "orders" is not a shade less after two decades of intensive and almost continuous study and discussion under the most friendly and favorable conditions. There is vastly more mutual understanding and appreciation, but there have been no conversions from one position to another.

The formal statements issued by the Faith and Order conferences and by the assemblies of the World Council of Churches have repeatedly and sincerely deplored the "sin of division" and have recognized that communions are separated not only by their theologies but also by "preoccupation with our internal affairs" and by being "too much dominated by ecclesiastical officialdom, clerical or lay" (quoting Amsterdam's Section I), but the discussion inevitably centers on the theological differences which stubbornly resist all efforts to resolve them into agreements.

One cannot avoid the impression that the most influential and articulate leaders of the ecumenical movement are proceeding on the assumption that the attainment of a united Church waits upon the achievement of general theological agreement, though this is often called "unity on the truth." This is the clear implication of many utterances that are weighty either with official sanction or with the great prestige of their authors.

In an article under the title "Various Meanings of Unity" in the *Ecumenical Review* (October, 1955) Dr. Visser 't Hooft expresses surprise that so many people do not yet know that "we [of the World Council] believe that doctrinal relativism is not an ally but rather a danger for true ecumenism." The phrase "doctrinal relativism" is somewhat enigmatical, but in any case it would seem to be the opposite of doctrinal absolutism. The implication is that the formulation of an absolute doctrinal standard is essential to true ecumenism.

The same author in the same article summarizes certain official statements in the reports of the Edinburgh, Amsterdam, and Evanston conferences as declaring that "full church unity must be based on a large measure of agreement in doctrine." The entire article stresses the thought that the "only unity we are concerned with is unity in obedience to truth," and that therefore the churches and the World Council of Churches must engage in "serious theological study" to discover the truth upon which unity is to be based. In this context discovery of the truth upon which unity is to be based clearly implies that the discoverers must come to agreement upon what would necessarily be a somewhat extended statement of doctrine and practice covering the main points upon which churches and Christians have hitherto been divided by their differences. The passages of the reports cited in the article fairly support the summary, and its accuracy as reflecting at least one important line of ecumenical thinking is confirmed by much other documentary evidence.

An Outline of Preparatory Studies, issued in anticipation of the North American Conference on Faith and Order, called to meet at Oberlin, Ohio, in September, 1957, lists the following questions, among others, as appropriate for consideration by the sixteen regional study groups organized in preparation for this conference:

What degree of consensus in faith is already realized? At what points do the most serious conflicts in the realm of doctrine arise?

Among our churches there is greater mutual recognition of one baptism than of one Eucharist. What are the implications of this recognition for our division at the Lord's table?

Has ecumenical conversation arrived at the point where we should attempt a common statement concerning the active presence of our Lord in Holy Communion?

How may we rightly distinguish between that *order* which is essential to the church's life and that organization where flexibility and diversity are desirable?

Where may we locate the actual centers of authority and freedom in existing polities—Congregational, Presbyterial, Episcopal?

Without a doubt the co-operative study of these questions will be a rewarding experience for every participant. It would, however, be a wholly unprecedented event if even a single one of the "serious conflicts in the realm of doctrine" were resolved into an agreement or if—to take an example at random—a single Lutheran and a single Disciple of Christ, having entered upon this study with the views characteristic of their respective communions, were to emerge with a "common statement" of the nature of Christ's presence in the bread and wine of the Eucharist. And yet, in view of the reiterated declaration that unity must be based on the "truth" and that it requires a "large measure of agreement in doctrine," it can scarcely be doubted that these questions were set before the regional study groups in the hope that they would make appreciable progress toward finding generally acceptable answers so that there might be at least a beginning of the removal of the theological roadblock that is said to bar the road to unity.

It is especially significant that the theme of the Oberlin study conference is "The Nature of the Unity We Seek." It may make an important contribution if it adheres to that topic, rather than accepting the presupposition that the unity we seek must be one of uniformity in doctrine, polity, and worship, and then spending its efforts in a vain endeavor to formulate agreements on all these things or in divising ingenious theological double talk which might temporarily conceal the still existing differences. This book is being written at a time when the Oberlin conference is still some months in the future, so I can only speak hopefully of what that conference may do if it clearly perceives the real issue which is presented by its announced theme, and if it then realizes that the pressing problem is not to find or formulate an extended and universally acceptable body of doctrine to serve as a basis of union, but to come to some decision about the *nature* of the unity we seek and the *character* of a future united Church. It may be that the nature of the unity we ought to seek—and of the only kind of unity that can be sought with the slightest reasonable hope of ever finding it—would not require any such "large measure of agreement in doctrine" as has been generally supposed or such as has been eagerly sought through all these years of intensive ecumenical theological conference.

By this time it is certainly no secret from any reader that throughout this book I have been pamphleteering in favor of a kind of church unity which could include communions having the widest possible variety of doctrines, polities, and forms of worship and individuals holding a wide range of theological opinions.

Faith and Order has often seemed to lean strongly toward a concept of essential unity embracing varieties of opinion and practice, but always with reservations or ambiguities in its expression. More than once at the Edinburgh Conference (1937) the report of a section would give a descriptive account of the disagreements in its field and then end by saying (in substance): "We do not find in these differences any justification for continued separation." Yet the limits of tolerance were soon reached. The final report included what amounted to the recommendation of a doctrinal formula which might be used as the test of a church's fitness to be counted among the Christian communions:

We acknowledge the Apostles' Creed and the Creed commonly called the Nicene, as witnessing to and safeguarding the faith, which is continuously verified in the spiritual experience of the Church and its members—remembering that these documents are sacred symbols and witnesses of the Christian faith rather than legalistic standards.

Every creed is by the very nature of creeds and the meaning of the word a witness to the faith. The formulation by Athanasius was a witness to the faith; and so also was the formula of Arius which the Nicene Council rejected; and so were the Augsburg and Westminster Confessions and the Thirty-nine Articles, though the adherents of no one of these would accept either of the other two; and so was the Racovian Catechism, which was rejected by all the great groups of Protestants. It must be the common faith of Christians that it said to be "continuously verified by the spiritual experience of the Church"; certainly that could not apply to the Nicene metaphysics of the divine "substance" or to its crucial *homoousion*. It is not easy to see how a "standard" of correct doctrine can accomplish its intended purpose unless it is "legalistically" applied. It may be that the intention was to indicate that, while this is acknowledged to be the standard of complete orthodoxy, it should be permissible to extend Christian fellowship to include some who are not willing to be bound by its terms.

There are two things wrong with any arrangement by which a united Church might adopt this or any other creed as the official "symbol" of its faith and yet not apply it as a criterion of qualification for membership. The first is that the very word "symbol" in its proper historical meaning denotes a badge or distinguishing mark by which a person or group wearing it can be identified, as a Roman soldier in a certain legion could be known as such by wearing the legion's symbol. This was the sense that came over into Christian usage. One who professed the Christian faith could be distinguished from non-Christians or heretics by his affirmation of the proper creed (the Nicene after 325) which was its accredited symbol. For the Church to adopt a symbol and not use it as one is to invite the evasive explanation, "We don't say it, we only sing it," and to leave still unanswered the question as to what is the *real* standard of fitness for recognition as a Christian or as a Christian communion. The second thing that is wrong with

212

this procedure is that it establishes a class of substandard Christians, a kind of halfway covenant. But no thoughtful and self-respecting Christian wants to be a member of a church which has a doctrinal standard that he cannot accept but which is willing to admit him merely as a concession and to avoid the odium of appearing to be too "legalistic" in the application of its own avowed criteria. Protestant churches do not approve the Catholic idea of an "implicit faith," which consists in agreeing in advance to believe whatever the church teaches or may hereafter teach, even though one may give no personal assent to the specific doctrines or even know what they are.

This Edinburgh action may perhaps be regarded as a parallel to that of the Evangelical Alliance, which adopted (1846) a doctrinal basis of nine articles which was later approved (1867) by the American branch, but added the declaration that

this brief summary is not to be regarded in any formal or ecclesiastical sense as a creed or confession, nor the adoption of it as involving an assumption of the right authoritatively to define the limits of Christian brotherhood, but simply as an indication of the class of persons whom it is desirable to embrace within the Alliance.

That was well enough as a statement of the qualifications for membership in a particular organization of Christians formed for a specific purpose, but that is something very different from describing the character of a united Church of which all Christians are to be recognized as members. The Evangelical Alliance never professed to be coextensive with the ecumenical Church.

Faith and Order, whether as an independent movement from Lausanne (1927) to Amsterdam (1948) or as a commission of the World Council of Churches since the latter date, has been definitely oriented toward ecumenicity. In its approach to that goal it has wavered between two attitudes—the quest of a general theological consensus as the doctrinal basis of a united Church and the generous impulse to find the way to a unity which would be consistent with doctrinal diversity. Its quest has for the most part been directed toward the first of these two objectives.

This ambiguous attitude is illustrated again in its latest pronouncement, the report of the Faith and Order section of the Second Assembly of the World Council of Churches at Evanston in 1954. Much is said in that report, and very properly, about the "sin of division," and there is an earnest call to penitence on that score; but little is said in the way of defining the sin that has caused and perpetuated the sinful state of a divided Church, and little to indicate who is guilty of it, whether those who originally caused the divisions or those who have inherited this condition and have not yet been able to decide what to do about it. In an organization many of whose participants had worked fraternally together for years there was, as might be expected, a general agreement that a certain amount of diversity in the Church is natural and harmless, provided it does not "disrupt the unity of the Body." For example, paragraph 15 of the Report of Section I:

There is diversity which is not sinful but good because it reflects both the diversities of gifts of the Spirit in one Body and diversities of creation by the one Creator. But when diversity disrupts the manifest unity of the Body, then it changes its quality and becomes sinful division.

The first of these two sentences refers to a "diversity of gifts" which, unless the historic meaning of the phrase is badly distorted, has no relevance to the kind of diversity under consideration. The Church has never been divided because to one member is given the gift of prophecy, to another the gift of healing, to another divers kinds of tongues; nor can different understandings of the mind of Christ and the teachings of Scriptures about sacraments, "orders," polity, and doctrine be intelligently brought under the category of

214

"diverse gifts of the Spirit." The second sentence seems to assume that division is the automatic result of some special and sinful kind of diversity which is to be distinguished from the nonsinful kind by the fact that it does not come from "diversity of gifts of the Spirit." The effect is to give a misleading impression of tolerance for "diversities" while excluding from this amnesty all those that really matter in relation to the unity of the Church, and to stigmatize as sinful those differences of judgment or interpretation—different, that is, from the "main body" of the church—which have given occasion for division. Yet it is stated in paragraph 6 of the same report that "divisions in the Church have been caused and are perpetuated, to a large degree, by a sincere concern for the gospel," and a deserved tribute is paid to the noble service rendered by the "separated" saints in many communions whose ministry God has owned and has used "to save souls, to build up communities who worship Him, and to preserve or recover aspects of His truth."

The original "working paper" which was before the Faith and Order section at Evanston when it began its deliberations contained some searching sentences which were eliminated in the course of drafting and redrafting the report—and just as well, for they were in advance of the thinking of the section:

> Moreover, the Holy Spirit has bestowed gifts upon us as individuals. These diversities produce a rich variety of congregations, ministries, forms of church life and government. But they are given for the fullness of the Church and the glory of God. They provide no justification for actual separation.

Aside from the point mentioned above—that there is no historical, theological, or psychological ground for saying that the various opinions about church polity, orders of the ministry, and sacraments grew out of a diversity of gifts bestowed upon individuals by the Holy Spirit—this gives a clearer recognition of the true character of a united Church than has been registered in any official Faith and Order paper. Whatever their origin, these variant convictions about sacraments, orders, and polity, together with the theological diversities that might well have been mentioned along with them, are precisely the things that *are* generally held to necessitate and justify division.

The total import of this Faith and Order report, as of most of the serious thinking that has been done in the ecumenical movement, tends to support these two propositions: first, that diversity of opinions about doctrine, polity, and orders is not in itself sinful; second, that division in the Church is sinful. Since the diversity is obviously the occasion for the division, it seems an inevitable conclusion from these premises that it is sinful to make diversity of opinions and practices a ground of division. Where else can the sin of division lie? If the differences are inevitable and not sinful, and if division is sinful, then the locus of the sin must lie in sinfully dividing over nonsinful differences.

Such recognition of the specific nature of the "sin of division" cannot fail to contribute to the spiritual health of ecumenically minded Christians as well as to the clarity of their thinking about the nature of unity and the way to attain it. It is confusing and frustrating to be frequently exhorted to penitence for the "sin of division" and to be constantly and properly reminded that a divided Church "stands under the judgment of God," if one has no clear idea of the nature of the sin of which one is expected to repent or the extent of one's participation in it, and therefore no clear idea as to what can be done to put away that sin. If penitence is to be more than an unhappy state of mind or a general sense of unworthiness and finitude in the presence of the Infinite and Eternal—and still more if it is to be, as true penitence must be, a godly sorrow for one's own sin and not an indictment of other people for theirs—it must lead to a program of action directed toward putting away the acknowledged sin and remedying the wrong condition which it has induced. A penitent thief stops stealing and begins to make restitution. A penitent drunkard stops drinking and sobers up. The word of forgiveness to every penitent sinner is "Go, sin no more." What then shall penitent Christians or churches do if they truly repent of a "sin of division" which consists of dividing over diversities of doctrine and practice which are not in themselves sinful?

The answer to that question is too obvious to require statement. Those who honestly believe that division in the Church is sinful and who feel enough responsibility for causing or perpetuating it to warrant a profession of penitence will seek to unite as quickly and fully as possible with all other Christians regardless of the differences which have sinfully been made the grounds of separation from them. This is in my judgment precisely the course that will have to be taken if a united Church is ever to become a concrete reality.

This does not, of course, solve the whole problem. No more can be claimed than that it indicates the direction in which unity is to be found and the "character of a united Church" when and if unity is ever attained. It will be a Church exhibiting wide varieties of doctrine, structure, orders, and cultus. Two questions, or groups of questions, remain.

First, what is to be done about those communions which hold as essential to true churchliness some point or points which other Christians do not so regard, and which therefore are not willing to merge with a united Church in which these points are not unanimously accepted? Such points might be the primacy and infallibility of the bishop of Rome, or the Eastern Orthodox liturgy, or the historic episcopate, or the presbyterial polity; or congregational independency, or immersion, or the real presence of Christ's body in the Eucharist, or the trinitarian formula of the Nicene Creed. The answer is that nothing can be done to bring into a united Church any of those large portions of the Church which not only adhere to these doctrines and practices but insist that they must be accepted by the whole Church as a condition of union. Nothing, that is, except continuously to leave the door open for them to enter the united Church, bringing their specific ideas and practices with them if they will but not forcing them on other Christians or unchurching those who do not accept them. If they cannot unite on those terms, then they cannot unite. This will mean, of course, that there will not be a completely united Church until they do enter it. That may be a long time, but it would be futile to make compromises which would please some and exclude others. It is an absolute essential of the union of Christians in one Church that no one be required to accept something that he does not believe—or be excluded for not accepting it—in order to satisfy the demands of some influential party which may insist that its particular doctrine or polity is of the essence of the faith or of the *bene esse* of the Church. Such a compromise if skillfully devised might produce a supersect, but also it might block the road to a wider unity for the next hundred years.

The other question is, How is such a united Church to function, and what are to be the visible signs of its unity? It has been generally recognized and often affirmed by promoters of the ecumenical cause that it is one thing for the Church to *be* united and another thing for its unity to be *manifested*. This valid distinction has sometimes been emphasized to the point of declaring that already we really *are* one Church— "We are one in Christ," "The unity of the Church is a given unity"—so that the real problem is only that of finding adequate ways of manifesting the existing unity. There is truth in this, but a truth from which wrong inferences may easily be drawn. The Church "in God's design" (to use the Amsterdam phrase) is indeed one. The Church as a divine creation, or as a mystical entity, cannot be two or ten or an indefinite number; it can only be "intentionally and essentially" one. The Church as the total fellowship of believers ought to be one, and it actually has more unity than it uses or exhibits. Beneath its obvious divisions and the isolation of its parts from one another in their normal activities in ordinary times, there is a substratum of common faith and mutual concern which manifests itself, inadequately but unmistakably, in times of

218

stress and trial. The Church considered as the whole company of believers needs more unity than it has—that is, more love, more fellowship, more bearing of one another's burdens, more participation in one another's joys and sorrows, more concerted action in common causes. These things are not merely manifestations of unity; they are constituent elements of the Church's unity. We do not get to the bottom of the trouble if we say that, since we are already "one in Christ," all we now need to do is to devise more adequate ways of manifesting that unity. The Church needs both a closer unity than it now has *and* a fuller manifestation of it.

The erroneous inference that may be drawn is that the needed manifestation of unity is merely, or chiefly, an extension of the ways in which the Church and its many separated parts have tried to manifest their unity in ages past—that is, by uniformity in doctrine, worship, polity, and "orders." The quest for unity, which has been traced historically in several chapters of this book, has been a quest for these kinds of visible and institutional manifestations of unity, usually on the assumption that unity could not exist without such manifestations. It has been shown that these broke down even when they were supported by pressures amounting to persecution and that they never even approximated success without such pressures. They became, in fact, not manifestations of unity but the chief grounds of division. The case is no better if, on the assumption that an underlying unity already exists independent of the visible phenomena of church life, we are now tempted to use these discredited methods as the means of manifesting that unity. In the light of the witness of history it would be an inexcusable folly for the ecumenical impulses of our time to dissipate their energies in a fruitless endeavor to promote and manifest unity by adopting those tokens and criteria of unity which have never been anything but divisive.

No one whose view of the world-wide state of the churches is in even the slightest degree realistic can entertain the illusion that their union on any terms is just around the corner.

Even if their leaders who meet in ecumenical conferences were to come to agreement on a satisfactory basis of union, their constituencies would still need an extended course of preparation for the event. Both processes will be long and tedious. There is no danger of the churches being stampeded into union on terms not generally acceptable—or on any terms. Nevertheless, though the goal is distant, it is important that the leaders in the movement keep their eyes fixed on the right goal and choose a road that goes in that direction, and that they do not, under the influence of powerful voices or impressive delegations in ecumenical assemblies, circle back into blind alleys which have never led to anything except division.

As long ago as 1923 at a British Evangelical Congress a representative of the Church of Scotland, Norman Maclean, declared that there are "three roads along which we *cannot* hope to arrive at union." As he enumerated them, these three roads were: unity of doctrine, a common theory of church government based on a theory of church orders, and uniformity of worship and rites.[3]

One result of a possible insistence upon that "large measure of agreement in doctrine" which Dr. Visser 't Hooft regards as the voice of the Edinburgh and Amsterdam conferences would be to bar out any whose theology is in any sense "liberal." Perhaps that is the intention. Everyone who ever participated in any of the great ecumenical gatherings knows that their theological climate is definitely conservative. Any extended doctrinal statement that might conceivably be acceptable to the majority of such an assembly would certainly exclude every kind of liberalism. Creeds have always been framed largely for the purpose of shutting out those who deviated from the orthodoxy of the framers. Without stopping to argue the matter I will only say that in my judgment a "united Church" which has no room in it for liberals would no more be a real united Church than is the Roman Catholic Church, which calls itself the whole

[3] The address is published in E. R. Ingham, *Christian Unity and the Gospel* (London: Hodder & Stoughton, 1924).

Church while having no room for those who do not submit to the authority of Rome. Liberal Christianity is not the outmoded intellectual fashion or the negligible factor in Christianity today that many would like to think. United fundamentalism, under whatever name, would not be the united Church.

Even if a conservative union were formed of such magnitude as to give the impression of being the main organ of Christianity and were to call itself the united Church, this would have the disastrous effect of alienating the Church, even more than it is now alienated, from the intellectual and cultural movements of the modern world. Reinhold Niebuhr, whom no one will accuse of being prejudiced in favor of liberalism, contributed an article to a series in the *Christian Century* under the title "What Kind of Unity Do We Want?" On this point he said:

The ecumenical movement is not explicitly orthodox; but the general presuppositions of the worldwide church certainly give stronger support to a traditional orthodoxy than to any formulation of the Christian faith which is partially determined by the disciplines of modern culture—which therefore takes Bultmann's questions about the nature of the kerygma seriously, even though it may not agree with his answers. At any rate, the general influence of ecumenical relations is to subordinate those questions about history and the history of "God's mighty acts" in Christian revelation which embarrass the more uncritical believers.

The net result of this tendency must be to widen the chasm between the Christian faith and the modern mind at the precise moment when the modern man is shaken in the alternatives to the Christian faith which he once took for granted. But he presumably remains a modern cultured man, who has scruples about believing incredible "facts"; and he probably finds those very facts, which some desire as validation of the gospel, hazards to true belief. But he is not deaf to the essential kerygma, which is that "God was in Christ reconciling the world unto himself." Religious purity is, in short, related to historical honesty. Surely this is a treasure of "liberalism" which we cannot discard and which, if discarded, we must restore.[4]

We come at last to the question as to what the united Church will be like if it has within its membership Christians of all the various denominational traditions and all shades of theological opinion, if it does not practice a uniform mode of worship in all its congregations and communities, and if it does not have a comprehensive and integrated system of polity to give it visible institutional unity. The honest answer is that I do not know how it would work out. It has never been tried under conditions anything like those of our time. No one knew how the United States was going to work out when the founding fathers initiated that splendid and daring experiment, but they had a deep conviction that certain principles were right, and they believed that right principles had a better chance of success than wrong ones. There are certain principles concerning the Church, its fellowship, its faith, its freedom, and its unity, that are right. It is the business of the Church to discover these principles and to see to it that they work. In writing this book I have tried to trace the history of the concept of unity and the methods employed in attempting to maintain or restore unity, and so to discover what kinds of attempted unity have consistently failed and what the character of a united Church must be. Only future experience can determine the patterns of its future operations. When the churches have arrived at the point where they are willing even to *try* to live as one in harmony and unity, still having all the diversities that have hitherto divided them, then the problem of *how* they shall live as one will already be more than half solved.

In November, 1951, a small conference was held at the Chateau de Bossey, near Geneva, under the sponsorship of the Faith and Order Commission, to prepare some materials for

[4] May 23, 1956, p. 641. Used by permission of the *Christian Century*.

the Lund Conference of 1952. One paragraph of the report approved by this conference reads as follows:

Some look back with longing to a past when a very high degree of unity appeared to exist within the Church. A closer examination, however, reveals the unpleasant fact that in the attainment of this unity coercion or persecution played a lesser or a greater part. Sometimes the Church was supported by the strong arm of the state in enforcing unity; sometimes it applied physical and spiritual coercion itself; sometimes the state applied the coercion in its own interests. This fact carries with it far-reaching implications for the type of unity which can be reached under conditions of civil liberty. No one participating in ecumenical discussions would defend the use of any form of coercion in attaining unity to-day, because unity must grow out of the message of Jesus Christ. Our quest is for such unity as is compatible with freedom.

I would be willing to end on that note—especially since I wrote the original draft of that paragraph, in a somewhat stronger form—but I will risk adding as an epilogue to the entire argument a specific summary of some characteristics which, as it seems to me for the reasons indicated in these chapters, the Church must have if it is ever to be a truly united Church of believers exercising their liberty as Christians and as citizens of the modern world. This is not a blueprint but an indication of what appear to be the implications of "such unity as is compatible with freedom."

1. The members must love one another and feel that sense of brotherhood and mutual concern for one another's spiritual and temporal welfare without which no "church," whether local, denominational, or universal, can be truly a Church. This is the one indispensable element.

2. There must be an interchangeable membership. A member of any congregation must upon application be acceptable as a member of any other congregation without tests or conditions other than evidence of his previous membership. If a member anywhere is not a member everywhere, the Church

would not be one Church. A member can select his local congregation; a local congregation cannot select its members.

3. There must be an interchangeable ministry. A minister accepted as such in one part of the Church must not be considered in another part as disqualified for lack of some special kind of ordination or ecclesiastical authorization not required of the ministry generally. There must be no talk about "irregular ministries" when referring to any whose work is acknowledged to be acceptable to God but who have not had what some consider the proper hands laid on them with the proper form of words. But this does not mean that every minister would be an acceptable pastor for any congregation. It is not so now in any denomination. Congregations have the right to have ministers adapted to their needs and views, and such adaptation includes episcopal ordination if the congregation has convictions that require it.

4. Varieties of organization and structure must exist independently but harmoniously within the united Church, since its unity cannot be one of ecclesiastical government. No form of organization is excluded except such as would by their nature or their claims exclude all others. The coexistence of different polities would mean that not all congregations would be within the same institutional framework. The fact that the united Church cannot be a monolithic structure does not imply that it must be an amorphous mass. Organizations are needed, but they are not what unites the Church. Any attempt to blend into one uniform system the episcopal, presbyterial, Methodist, and congregational polities, with a view to making the acceptance of this composite structure a condition of participating in the United Church, would be self-defeating. It would be open to the same objection as would an effort to impose any of the polities mentioned—namely, that it would rule out those who on grounds of conviction could not accept it. There is no reason why these different polities should not continue to exist, each with its own constituency. Even in a united Church there will inevitably be closer association among

congregations having the same polity than among those not so linked. Some parts of the united Church might continue their relationship with governments if they could do this without pretensions of superior "churchliness." Again we must remind ourselves that, if unity does not consist in owing allegiance to the same synod, or convention, or bishop, or conference, then it will not be broken by the absence of this tie.

5. There will be no creedal or doctrinal test either for lay members or for the ministry other than the primitive test of loyalty that was embodied in the declaration "Jesus is Lord." The test cannot be less if the united Church is to be the Christian Church. To establish other criteria of orthodoxy on the basis of theologies that have developed in the course of the Church's history would be, as it has always been, to fence some Christians in and other Christians out, and so to divide the Church.

6. There must be similar liberty, and there will be similar variety, in the use and interpretation of the sacraments. It would be fatally divisive to insist upon the universal adoption of the "primitive practice" of the immersion of penitent believers as the only proper baptism (though I think it is), because not all Christians agree that this was always the primitive practice or that, if it was, Christ's intention was that this should be a permanent law for the Church. Similarly there must be room for different administrations and understandings of Holy Communion. Intercommunion should be possible even among those whose interpretations of the sacrament are quite different. Congregations wishing to employ other practices which they regard as valid sacraments should have full liberty to do so.

7. Equal freedom will be enjoyed by congregations for the use of various forms of worship, liturgical or nonliturgical. Neither the use of historic rituals and vestments nor abstention from their use can be mandatory. Congregations must have full liberty to worship in accordance with their convictions, tastes, and habits. Undoubtedly most of them will go on doing just

as they have done in the past, but with a greater sense of freedom to learn something from one another now that they have the fraternal feeling of all being in one Church, so that the contributions of each part are available to all. Congregations which prefer a liturgical (or nonliturgical) service will be within their rights in wishing to have like-minded ministers skilled in conducting such services.

8. There must be agencies of co-operation. Unity would be unreal if there were no effective channels of fellowship on a more than local scale or functioning agencies for the missionary, benevolent, and educational work of the Church. A united Church would not hold, or deserve, the respect of its own members or of the world if it were not effective in promoting those ends for which the Church exists. Some of those ends cannot be effectively promoted without the co-operative activity of many congregations. This co-operation must necessarily be voluntary as to its forms and the specific agencies which each congregation or individual will choose. When one thinks of the magnitude of a united Church, or even of that part of it that is in a single country such as the United States, it is evident that only the distribution of its influence and funds among many agencies could prevent a dangerous concentration of power in the hands of ecclesiastical administrators. The Church must have machinery in order to do its work. The Church should be united; the machinery need not be and is less liable to abuse if it is not. There is no contradiction in this, for the unity of the Church does not consist in the unity of its machinery. It consists essentially in the fulfillment of the first of the conditions enumerated above—namely, that the members love one another and constantly think of one another as being members of the same Church and have a sense of fellowship in sharing a common responsibility for carrying on throughout the world the work that Christ committed to his Church.

Liberty is essential in a united Church, but liberty is not in itself a bond of unity. A common loyalty, mutual love, and the recognition of shared responsibility are both the bonds and the evidences of unity. These are stronger bonds of unity than the uniformities and conformities upon which the churches have hitherto relied too much, and by resistance to which the Church has been divided. These qualities of love and service can be strong enough to bind the Church together and give substance to the saying that we are "one in Christ." They can be so clearly visible against the contrasting background of a selfishly competitive society that both the quality of Christianity and the unity of the Church will be made manifest, "that the world may believe."

INDEX

229

231

234

236

Index